For

[...]

Lynn Watkins

March 2008

CW00601447

Dylan Thomas & Vernon Watkins

PORTRAIT OF A FRIENDSHIP

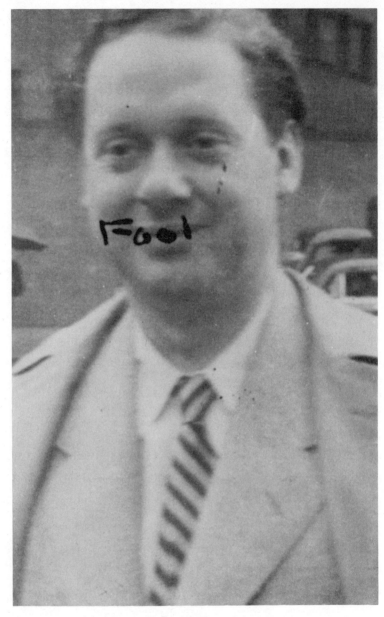

Frontispiece
"... A bulging Apple among poets ..."

Dylan Thomas & Vernon Watkins

Portrait of a Friendship

GWEN WATKINS

University of Washington Press

Seattle

Copyright © 1983 by Gwen Watkins

Printed in the United States of America

All rights reserved. No part of this publication may be reproduced or transmitted
in any form or by any means, electronic or mechanical, including photocopying,
recording, or any information storage or retrieval system, without permission in
writing from the publisher.

Library of Congress Cataloging in Publication Data

Watkins, Gwen.
  Dylan Thomas and Vernon Watkins.

  Reprint. Originally published: Portrait of a
friend. Llandysul, Dyfed: Gomer Press, 1983.
  Includes index.
  1. Thomas, Dylan, 1914-1953—Friends and associates.
2. Watkins, Vernon Phillips, 1906-1907—Friends and
associates.   3. Poets, Welsh—20th century—Biography.
I. Title.
[PR6045.A825Z94 1985]   821'.912   84-23428
ISBN 0-295-96205-4

For
TRISTAN
without whom I should still
be typing with one finger
through Chapter One

CONTENTS

LIST OF ILLUSTRATIONS

ACKNOWLEDGMENTS

This book could not have been written without the hundreds of pages of poetry and prose that Vernon Watkins wrote about Dylan Thomas. Wherever in *Portrait of a Friend* a quotation is used without ascription, it comes from this mass of material.

I am grateful to Dorothy Fox, O.B.E., Vernon's sister, and to Eric Falk, his lifelong friend, for their accounts of Dylan and Vernon in the early years of their friendship; and to J. C. Wyn Lewis for giving me his memories of that time, and especially for his detailed account of Dylan's visit to Cambridge. I am particularly grateful to Francis Dufau-Labeyrie, who made available to me, and allowed me to quote from, the whole of the invaluable correspondence between Vernon and himself, and who has besides assisted me with information which I should have found it difficult to obtain from any other source.

Dr. Ruth Pryor has kindly allowed me to make use of her bibliography of the works of Vernon Watkins.

My thanks are due also to the many people who have allowed me to quote from their letters: especially to Caitlin Thomas, Frances Richards (for permission to quote from Ceri Richards's letters), and Robert Hivnor, but also to Georges-Albert Astre, the late John Berryman, David Higham Associates Ltd., James Laughlin, Barbara Holdridge and Marianne Mantell of Caedmon Records, Charles Monteith and Peter du Sautoy of Faber and Faber, and the late Lady Snow.

Acknowledgments must be made to:
J. M. Dent and Sons Ltd., and the Trustees of the Copyrights of the late Dylan Thomas for extracts from *Quite Early One Morning* and *The Collected Poems of Dylan*

Thomas; to the above and Constantine FitzGibbon for extracts from *The Life of Dylan Thomas* and *Selected Letters of Dylan Thomas;* to the above and Faber and Faber Ltd. for extracts from *Dylan Thomas: Letters to Vernon Watkins;* to J. M. Dent & Sons Ltd. and Dr. Daniel Jones for extracts from *My Friend Dylan Thomas;* to Hodder and Stoughton Ltd. and Paul Ferris for extracts from *Dylan Thomas;* to J. M. Dent and Sons Ltd. and John Malcolm Brinnin for extracts from *Dylan Thomas in America;* to Dr. B. W. Murphy for extracts from *Creation and Destruction: Notes on Dylan Thomas;* and to Sandro Mario Rosso, Editore Stampatore in Biella and Roberto Sanesi for an extract from *Taliesin a Gower: Su una Poesia di Vernon Watkins.*

Material has also been used from the following newspapers and periodicals: *Encounter, Lettres Françaises, Mercure de France, The Mexico City News, The National Review, The New York Times Book Review, The Observer, Poetry* (London), *Poetry, The Saturday Review, The South Wales Evening Post, The Spectator, Time Magazine, The Times, The Times Literary Supplement, Tribune, Truth* and the *Yorkshire Post.*

I am greatly indebted to J. C. Wyn Lewis for allowing me to reproduce the photograph on page 87, and to Roger Davies for his preparation of photographic plates.

I should like last of all to record my indebtedness to the editorial staff of the Gomer Press for their help, and to my indefatigable typist and adviser Tristan Watkins.

1983   *G.M.W.*

FOREWORD

One of the great literary friendships, and one of the most productive, was that of Dylan Thomas and Vernon Watkins, two of the finest poets of our time. The importance to Thomas of Watkins' support and example has been stressed by nearly everyone who has considered Thomas's work and life. We have in addition those marvellous letters which Thomas wrote to Watkins and which Watkins published after his friend's death. It is, perhaps, a measure of Watkins' feeling for Thomas that he kept all those letters, as he did every evidence of the relationship which was to be one of the most important in his life. That the friendship continued for Watkins even after Thomas's death can be seen by the way the older man publicly defended Thomas's work and reputation, unstintingly praised his poetry, wrote "hundreds of poems about Dylan welling up like blood from a wound", as Gwen Watkins says. Nobody could have been more selfless in the service of a friend. Indeed, so assiduous was he in his celebration of Thomas that some people—and perhaps Vernon was among them—saw him as important only because of his friendship with Thomas. This is to misunderstand the complementary nature of that friendship and to underestimate seriously the value of Watkins' work.

Vernon was apparently so gentle, so unfailingly courteous, so calm, that his personality lacked the unpredictable quality that made a drama of Thomas's life. It was easy to assume that this mild bank clerk, impractical and absent-minded, keeping his regular business hours, was a source of security for the raffish young Thomas. I certainly assumed this. I accepted the idea that Vernon was able to combine his steady, placid life with the writing of extraordinary poetry. It is the oversimple portrait we have all accepted, but this book presents quite another picture.

For the truth is, and it is recognisably the truth, has the feel of authenticity, that Watkins was a much more complex and demanding character. Gwen Watkins explores her husband's friendship with Thomas from her husband's side and a much more interesting figure emerges. For the first time we see the situation from Watkins' angle and it is not too much to say it is a revelation. It will certainly alter our assessment of the man and it should bring renewed general interest in his work. This is the portrait of a man who was no mild and gentle creature, but a passionate and often angry man, one who demanded the highest standards from those around him and was intolerant when they failed, a determined and confident man. It is not a portrait I could recognise at first, although I recognised its force and new truth.

Yet in some ways it had always been evident, had we looked. We should have known it from his work and the manner of his work. He pursued those unfaltering poems with firm and prolonged and unswerving purpose, knowing exactly what he had to do and allowing nothing to get in his way. And we should have known it from the way he played. If anything called him as strongly as poetry, it was probably some kind of ball game. He played hockey and cricket and tennis with utter seriousness and dedication, finding the same sort of satisfaction from a good forehand drive as he did from a good line or image. There was nothing mild or gentle or tolerant about him on such occasions, nothing uncertain. He was fierce and competitive. That, I now see, was the true man, the man Gwen knew and brings before us in these pages. I remember clearly the last time I saw him, his light, quick, positive climbing of the Gower cliffs, the rest of us, panting and heavy-limbed, behind him.

But in this portrait of a friendship, Gwen Watkins gives us much more than a true, surprising picture of her husband. She examines with the utmost sympathy and firmness the extraordinary strength of the friendship that began when the two men were young and didn't end until Vernon's death, and that examination will inescapably change our understanding of the men and their work. She also examines with unfailing care and knowledge Watkins' obsession with Thomas and his poetry. "Not a day passed," she says, "till his own death that he did not think of Dylan." Since that death Gwen Watkins has worked with the greatest devotion to keep her husband's work before us. She has done this with energy and skill, and very objectively. These qualities are to be found here in abundance. She has seen her husband whole and presents him with clear-eyed love.

Leslie Norris
Provo, Utah,
March 1983.

Dylan Thomas & Vernon Watkins

PORTRAIT OF A FRIENDSHIP

Dylan was so responsive a person where he found affinity in others that the number of biographies which might be written about him would almost equal the number of people he seriously and adequately met. No biography is complete. It is in the collision of these unwritten biographies, when true stories are told, rather than in the distance of popular legend, that the true figure emerges.

Vernon Watkins

CHAPTER ONE: FIRST MEETING

They have put another lunatic into my cell. D.T.

Not long after noon on a weekday in February 1935, a young bank clerk stood in front of the window of Morgan and Higgs' bookshop in Union Street, Swansea. He should not have been standing there: he had only an hour for lunch, and it would take him all that time to order his meal in Lovell's cafe, eat it, and run back to Lloyds Bank in St. Helen's Road. Sometimes it might take rather longer than usual, because when at last the harassed waitress arrived to take his order, he would say confidingly, "I think I should like it to be a surprise today."

Still he stood in front of the window, which was filled with poetry books—all copies of the same book. Inside the shop more copies were piled on a table. The bank clerk took a few hesitant steps to the door, then back to the street, where he stood looking at the window for a little longer. ("Time yet for a million indecisions.") At last he went into the shop and almost unwillingly began to look through one of the copies. Finally he put it down and hurried out without buying it.

He repeated the same performance for several days. It was not until Saturday afternoon, when he left the bank about two o'clock, if there were no errors in the check-up, that, after more vacillation, he bought the book and took it home to read.

The bank clerk was Vernon Watkins. He was twenty-nine, and had been writing poetry since he was seven: he had determined that none of it should be published until after his death. The book was *18 Poems* by Dylan Thomas, who was twenty-one, and the best bookshop in Swansea was full of his first book. Vernon was irritated and perhaps envious; besides, his mind was completely preoccupied by the poetry of W. B. Yeats, whom he considered the greatest living poet. He did not want to read the poems of any other living poet. Worst of all, he had for many years considered himself to be the only poet in Swansea, serving the Muse with devotion in the evenings and at the weekends, hearing lines of poetry in his head as he roamed the bays and headlands of South Gower. But here was another Swansea poet, so young that he could have had no time to court the Muse; he must have whistled carelessly and she had come obediently to heel.

Still, Vernon bought *18 Poems*, and read it. He knew good poetry when he saw it, but he made no move to meet the poet.

> Then I ran into his uncle, whom I had known as a child. He said, "You must meet Dylan. His poetry is all modern; but whatever is wrong with his poetry, there's nothing wrong with him." And he gave me his address.

This uncle was the Reverend David Rees, the former minister of the Paraclete, Mumbles, the church which Vernon's father and mother both attended when they lived near Mumbles, first at Rotherslade, then at Caswell Bay, before they moved to Pennard, on the Gower peninsula. David Rees was said by Dylan's mother to have told her that her son should be in a madhouse. His remark that there was "nothing wrong" with his nephew may have been an attempt to urge Dylan into what might be considered more reputable circles than those he habitually moved in when in Swansea. He must have had a firm conviction of Vernon's rectitude; he would hardly otherwise, knowing Dylan's way of life, have risked the possible debauch of his most respectable parishioners' son. The address that he gave was, of course, No. 5 Cwmdonkin Drive.

Vernon bought the book and visited the house. Only Mrs. Thomas was at home. She was to become very much attached to Vernon, and after Dylan's death wrote him letters signed, "with fondest love" and blessings, "Your very old friend". On this February day she was probably anxious and propitiatory. She must have had experience, in the rigidly class-structured Swansea of the thirties, of the attitudes of those who thought D. J. Thomas had married beneath him. Vernon's mother came from a minor county family and moved in county circles, his father was not only an influential bank manager but took pride in his family's ancestry; Vernon and his sisters had all been to public schools, he and his elder sister to Cambridge and Oxford respectively. The meeting arranged by Mrs. Thomas's brother-in-law was not what she was used to.

She need have had no fear that Vernon would turn out to be a snob. It was not that he ignored social differences, but that he did not know they were there to ignore. All his life he would introduce a charwoman to a J.P. with no suspicion that the introduction might be embarrassing to either; he would be as deferential—or, on rare occasions, as blazingly rude—to a pot-boy in an East-end pub as to a peer of the realm. When I became engaged to him, he invited me to tea at his billet in New Bradwell, and I tried to find out what sort of rooms he lived in and what his landlady was like. He was utterly unable to tell me. Until I arrived I had no idea whether I was to meet a clergyman's widow in reduced circumstances or a retired barmaid. (She turned out to be a kind sensible woman who had left school at the age of twelve and kept, on the meagre pension of a railwayman's widow, a goat, who had been unwillingly patted by the young Philip Larkin, and a daughter recently crossed in love, not for the first time, whom she described as ''a big, fond girl.'')

Mrs. Thomas said that Dylan was in London but expected home shortly, and promised that she should get in touch with Vernon soon after his arrival in Swansea. He did, in fact, telephone the day after, and they arranged to meet in Pennard, the village on the south Gower coast where Vernon lived with his parents.

I remember that first meeting very clearly. He was rather shy, but intense and eager in manner, deep-voiced, restless, very humorous, with large, wondering eyes, and under those the face of a cherub. It was a Saturday afternoon, and we went for a walk on the cliffs. We had not gone far when I realized that this cherub took nothing, either in thought or words, for granted, but rather challenged everything with the instinct of a stubborn nature guarding its freshly discovered truth . . .

I had written a great many poems before we met. On his first visit to me I read him three or four, and, when he asked if I had more, he was very much amused when I lugged a trunk into the room A great many of the poems were derivative in part, for they dated back a long way; but certain ones he liked, and he quickly showed me what was fresh in my work, and what was not.

So began a relationship for which it would be difficult to find a name. On Vernon's side it was like love at first sight, except that love, however idealistic, usually has at least a tinge of the erotic, and here there was no slightest hint of it: indeed, Vernon said that he found Dylan physically "slightly repulsive". But it was more than the bedazzle-ment of an exciting new friend with interests like one's own, for that fades naturally into the light of common day, and this never did: a meeting with Dylan held the same excitement for Vernon to their last meeting, just before Dylan left for America and death. Certainly part of the attraction lay in the fact that they both loved and practised the grand art, but Vernon was to meet other poets whom he admired, yet who did not call out this passionate allegiance. Vernon was naturally rather an assertive young man, highly critical of anyone who did not measure up to his exacting standards; what was it in Dylan or himself that made him all his life a satellite to this comet that blazed across his path, a giver of unconditional love to this "young Apollo" who cared nothing whether he was loved or not?

For I do not think that the friendship.meant very much to Dylan. What love he had to give was already given, to poetry and to his own Welsh childhood. Not even Caitlin could compete with those. It seemed to me that Dylan's friendships were always transient; he needed perpetual company, but I could never see that it mattered to him who he was with. He never seemed to need, or miss, indiv-iduals; indeed, he quickly got tired of the same faces, and would move away to seek new ones.

He certainly found in Vernon a devotion to poetry as intense as his own, and this was a novelty and a stimulation to him at first; this was the first time he had been able to read his own poetry to a listener who was willing to spend hours discussing a single line or even word, and I think this exhilarated him. He was willing to listen to Vernon's own poetry at first, and discuss it in detail, but he soon lost interest in this. He liked some of Vernon's poetry, and wrote to Oscar Williams in 1944 mentioning ''the lovely poems of my friend Vernon Watkins (who certainly should be published in book form in America)''. Constantine FitzGibbon heard him read *Portrait of a Friend* and *Ballad of the Mari Lwyd,* and he occasionally included some of Vernon's poems in his American readings; but I never got the impression that Vernon's poems were among his favourites, nor indeed that he knew very much about the books after the first, of which he had heard most of the poems read when they were still in manuscript.

There are very few references to Vernon in *Selected Letters of Dylan Thomas,* not more than ten lines out of more than four hundred pages of letters. A letter to Glyn Jones, shortly after the meeting which Vernon had found so spell-binding, said, ''It's very lonely here in Swansea and the few old friends I have spend their days in work and their evenings in indulging in habits which I've had quite enough of—at least temporarily.'' In a letter to Geoffrey Grigson a little later Dylan referred to the metre of a German poem he had translated. But he never knew any German, and it is impossible to recognise the metre of a German poem without that knowledge. Dylan must have taken the poem to Vernon, to get both the meaning and the metre; yet there is no reference to him in the letter.

Vernon always said that Dylan was very perceptive about character. I doubt this. Sensitive to his own effect on people he undoubtedly was, and he could intuitively adjust himself to the expectation of others; but I don't believe he could assess personality—or indeed that he was sufficiently aware of other people to know what they thought or felt. He once proposed that "Vernon should write the Glamorgan Lad, and tell how, one by one, we reach the gallows, the marriage bed, the grave, Harrow, Windrush or the Air Force." Had he really known Vernon for four years without realising that narrative verse was the one kind of poem he could never write? His sense of plot did not exist: he knew Tennyson's *Maud* almost by heart without ever realising that there was a "story" in it. And certainly Dylan's own estimation of Vernon's character "—the one happy person I know . . . who seems to be almost entirely uncomplicated . . . who has worked through all the beginnings and finds himself a new beginning in the middle—" was about as far from the truth as it could be.

Of Dylan's own letters to Vernon, thirty out of ninety are written to make a straightforward request: for money, for the loan of a suit, for the typing and immediate return of his own poems, for Vernon's help in the criticism or selection of poems for readings. Of the others, a large number describe his poverty—"I'm afraid we're much too poor to be able to come up to see you for a long time,"—or give news of occasions such as his marriage or the birth of his son, which he knew would elicit a material response from Vernon. After Vernon's marriage in 1944, there are only twelve letters, of which two are straightforward requests, and most of the others are notes either arranging meetings or in answer to letters from Vernon.

I do not think that Dylan wrote to Vernon only when he wanted something, but I certainly think that if Vernon had not so instantly given him what he asked or hinted for, the letters would not have been so frequent. The fact that the requests so often came in postscripts, or at the very end of letters might show that Dylan wanted to conceal from Vernon or himself or both, his real reason for writing.

He said in one letter that he found Vernon's criticism of his poetry ". . . the most helpful there is for me, and I want it to go on." Whether this was true, partly true or mere flattery it is difficult to tell: he also said, ". . . I refute your criticism from the bottom of my catarrh", and complained

that Vernon's "ear" was deaf to the logic of his poems.
Then again he begged Vernon to come immediately to
Laugharne; "I need you urgently to rewrite a poem with
me . . ." But I doubt whether Dylan ever needed anyone in
his life to rewrite a poem with him. It is much more likely
that he needed some money urgently, and knew that if
Vernon came to Laugharne he would get it. John Davenport commented, in a *Spectator* review of Dylan's letters
to Vernon, "How brilliant the old boy was at not letting
right hands know what left hands were doing!"

When the letters were published, many reviewers made
adverse comments about the requests for money; some
even seemed to think that Vernon had not edited them out
so that he would get a kind of spurious kudos from being
known to have lent Dylan money. Nothing could be
farther from the truth. Vernon's bank salary was small,
but he was living at home with his parents, and he had all
the necessities and a great many luxuries. Dylan often
lacked the bare necessities of life. There was no reason at
all why Vernon should not have given Dylan money and
other things. He made his point of view very clear in a
letter to the *Observer* in 1957: "I foresaw that lop-sided
comment might be made on these small items of borrowing, but I left them in. In their time and context they were
significant, mattering so much to him, and not at all to
me."

This was certainly true about money; but, sadly, where
the relationship was concerned the reverse was true. All
his life it mattered "so much" to Vernon, and not at all to
Dylan. People were important in Dylan's life only as far as
they gave him what he needed. Vernon gave him material
help in some ways, he filled in some vacant hours, he did
introduce Dylan to some poets he hadn't known of (particularly French and German poets) and he did, at least at
first, amuse him. He had what Hugo Williams, in the
memorial volume, calls "a zany wit"; strange things happened to him, partly because of his own unawareness of
ordinary life, and Dylan was fascinated by his accounts of
the cockeyed events that were part of Vernon's daily liv-

ing. But eventually he ceased to need what Vernon could supply, and had little further use for him. To Vernon, however, Dylan was from the first, and always remained, a central figure in his life.

CHAPTER TWO: AFFINITIES AND SEPARATIONS

I did not expect, when I turned the pages of this book, that I should find in their author an affinity so much deeper than anything I can describe.
—V. W.

A possible question for a fantasy Eng. Lit. A-level paper (more fantastic, I mean, than even the questions set by the Examining Boards) would be: "Compare and contrast the lives of Dylan Thomas and Vernon Watkins." The similarities and differences make a curious pattern.

Both spent all the remembered years of their childhood in Swansea. Vernon came there when he was six; three years later Dylan was born there. They lived on different sides of the Uplands; Vernon to the south of Walter Road in Eaton Crescent, Dylan to the north in Cwmdonkin Drive. Both played over the same ground. In an article in the *Texas Quarterly* in 1961, Vernon wrote:

> The grass of the Recreation Ground can never compete with the boots that play on it. Brynmill Park, offering the olive leaf to doves and foxes, still holds its collection of incongruous cages. Cwmdonkin Park is as it was when Dylan Thomas wrote his poem *The Hunchback in the Park*, except that the reservoir is dry; it has changed little since I, too, played in it as a child. The lake of Singleton survives, undisturbed, the activities of builders. St. Helen's cricket ground is greener than ever. There are more policemen, but walls are still climbed, and although hoardings now hinder the spectators from the railway bridge, cricket matches are watched from houses with vulnerable windows, and the latest score seen from the tops of buses and carried round the coast.

Both children went to kindergarten in the Uplands; Vernon to St. Anne's in Gwydr Crescent, Dylan to Mrs. Hole's in Mirador Crescent. Dylan was the naughtiest boy in the school, Vernon the prize scholar who sat at a special desk studying Latin and covering himself with ink. Both schools gave little entertainments at the end of term, in which Dylan and Vernon took part. The child was very much father to the man in these performances. Dylan played to the gallery; instead of playing the sedate colonel he was cast as, he blew orange-peel through the newspaper he was supposed to be reading and rushed about the stage beating the air with his walking-stick, until the curtain came down. Vernon, taking part in a Dance of All Nations, missed his cue, and performed his anxiously-rehearsed Irish jig in slow motion to the mournful strains of an Indian dirge, carefully, though unconsciously, avoiding the arms stretched out from both wings to pull him off the stage. In both cases the entertainment was disrupted.

Both children spent their Saturday afternoons in the Uplands Cinema, known as the Itch-pit. In a broadcast called *The Place and the Poem* Vernon wrote of it:

> In the old days it used to be protected by a railing which seemed to have been built specially to keep the Saturday mob at bay. It was the time of the silent film, and the chief excitement every week was the serial, the short, horrifying serial, the serial which left every boy and girl gasping and yet hilarious when the words TO BE CONTINUED flashed upon a situation which knew of no continuation. At that moment the villain always had the upper hand. The walls of his trap-door dungeon were closing upon our hero and heroine, or knives were coming out of the walls all round them, leaving one space for the final knife to come, or they were on fire, or drowning in water which was gradually filling their cell. Logically they would die, and the funeral would be on Monday. Illogically they always just survived, and on the following Saturday we hailed their unexplained, hair-breadth escape.

Dylan wrote about it too, in *The Followers*:

> Week after week, for years and years, we had sat on the edges of the springless seats there, in the dank but snug, flickering dark, first with toffees and monkey-nuts that crackled for the dumb guns, and then with cigarettes: a cheap special kind that would make a fire-swallower cough up the cinders of his heart.

When he was ten, Vernon went for a year to the Grammar School, where Dylan was to pick up for a few years such education as he had. After that year, Vernon went away to prep. school and public school in England, but to him, as to Dylan, Swansea was always his heart's home, the immortal "ugly, lovely town".

> When I was away from Swansea . . . Dylan Thomas brought me home to it in a broadcast. It was near Christmas time, and he made all the buildings and streets come to life. It was as though he had pulled a cracker which contained a hat or a puzzle for everyone in the town.

Salzburg-on-the-Tawe Vernon called it; "never was there such a town as ours", wrote Dylan.

Both of them began to write poetry when they were children, and their descriptions of these early attempts show (given the differences of temperament) a remarkable similarity:

D.T.   . . . when I was very young, and just at school . . . in my eleventh year I read indiscriminately, and with my eyes hanging out.

V.W.   By the time I was ten I had collected most of the English poets . . . The hold which poetry had on my sensibility increased, and hardly ever relaxed its grip.

D.T.   I tumbled for words at once . . . out of them, out of their own being, came love and terror and pity and pain and wonder . . .

V.W.   Words in cadenced form, whether in rhyme or not, seemed to have an unrivalled power over the imagination. I was deeply moved by poetry, moved, I mean, to inexplicable tears by a pattern of words which seemed to me unforgettable.

D.T.   I wrote endless imitations, though I never thought them to be imitations, but, rather, wonderfully original things, like eggs laid by tigers.

V.W.   I wrote poems, and they usually reflected the style of the poet I was reading at the time. In language I was not at all precocious, only responsive. It made me confuse my own emotions with those of other poets, and write like them, only very much worse.

> D.T.　When I began to read . . . verses and ballads, I knew that I had discovered the most important things, to me, that could be ever . . . I knew, in fact, that I must be a writer of words, and nothing else.

> V.W.　I cannot remember a time when I did not mean to write poetry.

Vernon had one penchant that Dylan seems never to have had; he was fond of long poems:

> I thought Wordsworth's *Prelude* very good, but I discovered, by counting the pages, that Longfellow's *Tales of a Wayside Inn* was better. I had still to reckon up *Don Juan, In Memoriam* and *The Ring and the Book*, when I was already writing long poems myself in a note-book of epic dimensions. Here I must record that a rival poem of Tennyson's *Idylls of the King*, which was intended to be one line longer, was left unfinished at my prep. school . . . —a sad loss to English literature.

It is not surprising that, with this shared background, there should have been some affinity in what they wrote.

> We were drawn together partly because we were Welsh, partly because we were both religious poets, partly because we felt that a poem should be serious, and that a good poem was one which could never be fashionable. We particularly disliked 'clever' poems, the kind of poem in which a poet seems to say under his breath, 'How clever I was to find that way of putting it'. We both thought that the greatest rewards in poetry came to the poet when he was most receptive and dedicated, when his imagination was purged of everything but the humility and honesty of its real task; and we both knew that the labour and patience which waited upon those rewards belonged to a unique discipline.

''. . . We were both religious poets . . .'' This calm assumption entirely ignores the pitched battles of critics and biographers, from Aneirin Talfan's claim that Dylan was well on the way to Roman Catholicism when he died, to Paul Ferris's that religion was merely a stage-prop of his poetry. Vernon certainly, until after the war, believed that Dylan was a Christian poet, as he was himself; but this

was largely because Dylan knew and loved Job and Ecclesiastes, because they both loved the same religious poets,
such as Donne and Herbert, and because Dylan allowed
Vernon to read Kierkegaard to him while making appreci-
ative noises, which were probably sincere. I doubt very
much whether they ever talked about dogma, theology or
their own personal beliefs. (This would have been difficult
anyway: abstract discussion always worried Dylan, and
Vernon had in argument—like most Welshmen—what
Alfred Janes called ''a remarkable talent for always hitting
the nail on the point.'' I was keen on theological discussion, but I never had one with Vernon without concluding by telling him that he was a heretic, not an ortho-
dox Christian.)

Vernon later came to believe that Dylan too was, if a
Christian at all, a very unorthodox one. His note to Constantine FitzGibbon, after having read the manuscript of
FitzGibbon's *Life*, is probably as good a statement as any of
what he thought about Dylan's religious position:

> If he was, as I believe, religious and Christian, he doesn't
> need my advocacy, and if he wasn't he doesn't want it . . .
> Dylan recognised a great error in the Past and he saw ruin
> ahead . . . I would call Dylan a Blakean Christian but even
> that would be only an approximation.

All the same, I think that Vernon was intuitively right
about Dylan's being a religious poet—intuitively, because
his conviction rested not on evidence, but on his instinct
that Dylan felt as he himself did about God. They both felt
that the millions of wonderful things for poets to write
about had been made by some Power, and they both recognised very strongly that the power of the Word was
supernatural, and that praise was what was required by
whatever Power had made and kept the world. Vernon also
had a conviction, acquired during his breakdown, that he
had been saved from damnation by the sacrifice of
Another, whom he identified as Christ. Apart from this, I
think his faith in God was as nebulous and as certain as
Dylan's. In my opinion he is right to call Dylan a religious

poet, since he, no less than Vernon, expressed in his poems
a strong feeling of, and belief in, the numinous. "These
poems" said the Author's Note to the *Collected Poems*
". . . are written for the love of Man and in praise of God . . ."
It is a respectable restatement of the two great command-
ments "on which rest all the law and the prophets." Yet
Vernon also recognised that, whatever their affinity of
theme and attitude, there was a radical difference in the
poems they actually produced.

> . . . I recognised in Dylan Thomas a genius of a quite different
> kind which could do with words everything that I couldn't do
> with them; his writing was, I understood from the first, the
> exact complement of mine. I disliked every imitation of his
> work, but his own work I loved, for its unique mastery of
> texture. Like Hopkins, he always seemed to me a poet whom
> it was fatal to copy.

All this sounds as though the relationship were a purely
poetic one; had it been so, there would have been nothing
strange in the association of two poets, however different
in age or behaviour, meeting to discuss their craft, any
more than in the meeting of two musicians to practise. It
was the social and psychological elements which were
strange, and they were strange in different ways. Socially,
Vernon drew Dylan into his own orbit; psychologically, he
was drawn into Dylan's.

It is true that Dylan did invite him to the Wednesdays at
the Kardomah; he was rarely able to go to the Saturday
lunch-time meetings because, in the days when banks
were open on Saturday mornings, it was often two o'clock
before the staff could leave. But for the most part, when
Dylan was in Swansea or Bishopston, he and Vernon met
mainly at Pennard, where, when they were not reading or
writing poetry, Dylan was drawn into Vernon's usual pur-
suits; they took long windy walks, scrambled over the
rocks, went bathing, came back to Heatherslade to tea or
supper, played croquet in the summer or lexicon in the
winter. Although Dylan had been fairly active in his
youth, by 1936 walks were already 'unwonted' for him;

Vernon and Dylan at Laugharne, Autumn 1939

'. . . many, many thanks for the supersmart suit in which no moth-holes
could be seen . . .'

and as for bathing, Paul Ferris says that he "seems never to have gone *in* it [the sea], . . . on the Gower beaches where he went with friends as soon as he was old enough." There is no doubt, however, that Vernon's simple disbelief that any human being could be near the sea and not want to plunge in, did induce him to bathe occasionally, and even to say that he must do it more often. Sometimes he would sit on the beach throwing stones into the water while Vernon bathed. Dylan was amused at his new role, and called himself "your hearty, Britain-chested, cliff-striding companion." At the Heatherslade teas and suppers he was, according to Eric Falk, "a model guest", drinking tea or home-made lemonade, liking a glass of water by his side to sip at during the card games, always polite and pleasant to Vernon's parents and friends. Occasionally he would invite Vernon to tea at Cwmdonkin Drive or Marston (the house in Bishopston where his parents lived) and the same decorous scenes were enacted. It was no wonder that Mr. and Mrs. Thomas did all they could to encourage their dream of Dylan's becoming a respectable literary figure coming nearer to realization than it had ever been.

Dylan did not, in these early days, make any attempt to draw Vernon into his world of pubs and dives (if indeed he inhabited that world while he was in Swansea: a letter of 31 December, 1935 says, "I live a comfortable, sheltered, and now only occasionally boozy life in Swansea . . ."). They would sometimes have a drink after Vernon left the bank and then go back to Cwmdonkin Drive to spend the evening reading, writing and discussing poetry. "The poetry machine", Dylan continues in the same letter, "is so well oiled now it should work without a hitch until my next intellectually ruinous visit to the bowels of London".

Later, during the war and after, when it became impossible to see Dylan unless you went to a pub, Vernon did habitually meet him there; but in these pre-war days there is only one record of their spending the entire evening in a pub and both getting drunk.

Still, Dylan did his best to make it clear to Vernon that

however useful or pleasant he found this way of spending
his time, it was, for him, only a pastoral interlude:

> . . . the out-of-doors is very beautiful, but it's a strange
> country to me, all scenery and landscape, and I'd rather the
> bound slope of a suburban hill, the Elms, the Acacias, Rook-
> ery Nook, Curlew Avenue, to all these miles of green fields
> and flowery cliffs and dull sea going on and on. I'm not a
> country man; I stand for, if anything, the aspidistra, the prov-
> incial drive, the morning cafe, the evening pub . . .

And although he was polite about Vernon's way of life—
"you secluded in your Tower know and learn more of the
world outside than the outside-man . . ."—it must have
been increasingly plain to Vernon that although Dylan had
no objection to popping in to the Ivory Tower at intervals,
he neither could nor would stay there for long. But neither
this realisation nor Dylan's gradual loosening of whatever
bond there had been between them made any difference to
the intensity of Vernon's feeling for and about Dylan.

> "In the middle thirties", wrote Vernon in a note on his own
> poetry, "I bought an exercise book for making first drafts of
> poems. It was a school exercise book with mathematical
> tables and a map of England on the back . . . On the cover of
> this book I wrote against Name—Vernon Watkins, and
> against School—Romantic."

The same word most exactly describes his emotions where
Dylan was concerned. But though they were romantic,
even passionate, they contained no slightest tinge of the
erotic.

Dylan, however, may have mistaken the nature of Vernon's feelings for him, or at least may have mischievously
wanted to test them, since he proposed one week-end that
he, Vernon and Caitlin should all sleep in one bed. This
was the first weekend that Vernon stayed with the married
pair in Laugharne. They were then living in Gosport
Street, in the 'small, damp fisherman's furnished cottage'
found for them by Richard Hughes, and the double-bed
referred to by Dylan in a letter to Henry Treece as "a

swing-band with coffin'' was to be the scene of the temptation.

Dylan had been curious about Vernon's sexual life ever since they had met. At this time, and for years after, all Vernon's passion and intensity went into poetry; Dylan must at first have found that difficult to believe. Romantic feelings Vernon certainly had, but they were for poets; he wrote of one encounter:

> At the last sweetshop you would have kissed the maid, a beautiful Welsh girl but I only made her laugh while our lives flew for a moment into a mutual bit of butterscotch. It's no good. I cannot be romantic. I prepare the apple-pie bed for every likely customer, the tin mirror for all bright eyes.

His one love-affair (a purely unilateral one) was with Elizabeth Schumann, the celebrated soprano. On first hearing her sing, when he was a boy of nineteen, he had been so ravished that he had rushed to the stage door to offer her his hand and heart. That she was already married did not appear to him to be an obstacle to their union: such was his intensity of feeling that she could not help but return it. However, by the time he had hurried through the Cardiff shopping-arcades in a vain search for flowers to accompany his passionate declaration, the theatre was dark and the proposal was never made. But then and for many years after he remained faithful to the memory of his first love.

Whether Dylan thought Caitlin might tempt him from his fidelity, or whether he thought Repton had left its mark there is no way of telling: but he announced that there was only one bed in the cottage, and that it was large enough for them all. (Yet a few weeks later, he was writing to Henry Treece, ''There is a double bed in one room, two single beds in the other . . .'')

Throughout his life it never occurred to Vernon to doubt any statement (on any subject other than poetry) which might be made to him, as long as it was made with a straight face. Christopher Isherwood describes in *Lions and Shadows* how he and ''Chalmers'' convinced Vernon (in the character of "Percival") that they had made a new and highly sinister acquaintance:

> The gullible Percival believed all this, and was deeply impressed; but when Chalmers, carried away by his own improvisation, went on to describe how Moxon kept a cat in a birdcage and a canary flying free about the room, and when I added that he owned a large black serpent which accompanied him on rambles after dark, Percival began to smile reproachfully and murmured, in his deep musical tones, "Do you know, I believe you're ragging me?"

I myself persuaded him, when he was in his late thirties, to try Fry's Chocolate Spread on sardines, on the grounds that it was an ordinary recipe along the lines of *truite à l'amande*. He confided to me afterwards that he was surprised at its popularity, though he conceded that the flavour was "interesting". So it was not surprising that he accepted with complaisance Dylan's allotment of the sleeping space, and was only anxious to occupy it as soon as possible. It was the last day of a week's holiday from the bank, which he had spent cycling in North Wales; he had, he wrote to Francis Dufau-Labeyrie, "a sore bottom after doing eighty hilly miles" to Laugharne, he had been drinking beer at the pub, he had undergone an exhausting introduction to Richard Hughes, and he was ready for bed.

He therefore tumbled gladly into it, and was asleep before Caitlin came upstairs. Unfortunately he rolled into the hollow in the middle of the ancient mattress, and had to be awakened with the greatest difficulty by an anxious Dylan, who had to hold him up on one side of the slope while he himself clambered down into the dip. Vernon remembered waking at intervals throughout the night to hear Dylan cursing and groaning and Caitlin giggling.

This incident explains the otherwise cryptic remark in Vernon's letter to Francis about the weekend, "I stayed . . . with Dylan and Caitlin . . . Caitlin could cook, *wake up* [my italics], sew, clear away, wash up, light fires and do everything I thought she couldn't do." Whatever Dylan had hoped, or feared, to find out from the experiment remained buried, and the incident was never again referred to.

Vernon remained innocently under the impression that all overnight visitors were entertained by Dylan and Caitlin in this hospitable manner. "Would you like to go down one week-end with me?" he wrote to a friend. "We couldn't stay with them, though, as they can only put one person up." It was perhaps fortunate that he did not stay in Laugharne again until the Thomases had moved to Sea View, where he slept in the cardboard-bed which he was later to save from re-possession by a hire-purchase firm with the money he earned from *Life and Letters Today* for some poems about his godson Llewelyn.

It is doubtful whether Dylan ever did understand the nature of Vernon's feelings for him or indeed whether he cared to know. To Vernon himself they were probably not defined, but they were none the less intense and powerful.

The romantic and Arcadian world of youth, leisure, poetry and wit, had ended for Vernon with his breakdown. Henceforth he kept Poetry and the World at a distance from each other: he went to the Bank every day and wrote poems every night. (He said without resentment after he had retired from the Bank that no-one in Lloyds had ever shown the slightest interest in his poetry until he was awarded the Guinness prize; then, he said, they were interested in the £300 he had won, not in the poem.)

But now he had met a Poet, who, while rejecting the World in the shape of paid employment, had not retreated from it into an ivory tower but took it on its own terms. Vernon admired the man of the world, revered the poet, and appreciated the wit; but besides all this, he became, as several of his friends noticed, oddly protective about Dylan. Dylan was not to be criticized, was not to be held accountable for failures to keep appointments or other peccadilloes, was not to be forced, by the opinions of society or financial necessity, to abandon the daring, arduous but romantic life of living on and by poetry that he had chosen. Did Vernon feel guilty that he himself had lacked the courage to make this choice? At any rate, his own choice enabled him marginally to subsidise Dylan, and this he gladly and faithfully did. Dylan was a kind of *alter ego*, a poet who had taken the chance that he himself had baulked at.

It is unlikely that Vernon understood his own feelings for Dylan, or that he saw the situation in these terms. There was certainly a poetic affinity between the two, in that on the whole they liked the same kind of poems, but it was probably not as deep as Vernon thought. Dylan, like most Celts, was a shape-changer, and the shape he took was the one you wanted him to take: The "gusty man and a half" who ramped across America, "brandy and ripe in my bright, bass prime" was fulfilling the unconscious wishes of the prim and respectable academics who waited hopefully to be shocked. Vernon could never recognise this Dylan, and saw always the innocent behind the killing mask. It never occurred to him that the innocence might be a mask too.

Still, there was, I think, a real bond between Vernon and Dylan, though neither of them was conscious of it. They were like two travellers who started from the same place and arrived at a common meeting-place by very different routes, or like two scientists who solved the same problem by diametrically opposite methods. The two travellers, the two scientists meet for a short time; of course each wants to know how the other has arrived at this place, this solution. Dylan soon lost interest, but Vernon watched until his fellow-traveller reached the end of the way and then, going on himself, looked back again and again.

The unacknowledged, unadmitted, almost certainly unrealised bond between them was that both had chosen "perfection of the work" rather than of life.

Whether it is possible to choose both, who can say? It may be that the poet writes only because the need within him can be satisfied in no other way; but it must always, surely, be a very great temptation for a writer to turn to the struggle with words and away from the struggle with life. Words, after all, can be mastered, however agonising the struggle, and the result is permanent and satisfactory. The struggle with life, on the other hand (I mean, of course, the struggle to learn how to live and then to put that knowledge into practice) is equally agonising—though I sometimes think that poets don't realise this—and the results, if any, are seldom as satisfactory as a poem.

It must also be very easy for a poet to make the mistake of thinking that the successful struggle to write a good poem is identical with the struggle to mature. A good poem impresses the reader with its mastery of life; may not the poet be deluded into thinking that he has advanced as far in living as in poetry? Readers often suffer from this delusion too: it is why they are continually aghast that good poets are not always good men.

Dylan Thomas and Vernon Watkins were both good poets, Dylan perhaps a great one; but both developed and matured far more as poets than as men. It is difficult to see this lack of maturity as not in some way willed. Dylan wrote to Caitlin before their marriage

> . . . do you look like a real adult person, not at all anymore beautiful and barmy like the proper daughters of God? You mustn't look too grown up, because you'd look older than me; and you'll never, I'll never let you, grow wise, and I'll never, you shall never let me, grow wise, and we'll always be young and unwise together . . .

But to be childlike is one thing, to be childish another. The first is consistent with maturity, the last is not, and the difference between the two becomes more apparent as time passes. One is an acceptance of life, the other, after childhood itself is over, a retreat from life. There were elements of these qualities in the characters of both poets. Both liked (and indeed needed) to be 'looked after', neither was able, or perhaps willing, to cope with the practicalities of everyday life, neither could keep track of his possessions. ("Europe is littered with things I have lost", Vernon Watkins once said despairingly.)

Although Dylan is thought of as outgoing and talkative, and Vernon as reserved and sometimes withdrawn, they were both in fact very shy; they merely dealt with this shy-

ness in different ways. They found it difficult to talk un-
reservedly to each other (or, probably, to anyone else)
except on the subject of poetry, but this difficulty was
overcome by the continual use of humour.

> "In the parameter of conversation between close friends",
> says Owen Barfield, "a sustained ebullition of humour can
> perform two opposite functions. It can increase it by enabling
> intimate allusions which would be coarse or indelicate in any
> other form. But it can also arrest the progress of intimacy at a
> critical juncture, whether it comes as the unplanned inter-
> ruption by a ruling habit, or, used of set purpose, is raised like
> the traffic policeman's hand, gentler but not a whit less
> effective than the red light."

It can also be an oblique way of looking at reality, to make
it less real; something you can joke about can be made to
seem less frightening or less serious—and of course, the
wit can give life (which he can't control) a smack in the eye
with words (which he is very good at controlling).

So here again the dichotomy that was in their characters
appeared in their conversations: they talked about poetry
seriously, they talked about everything else humorously
or not at all.

Dr. Daniel Jones writes of his friendship with Dylan:

> Our natures, different as they were, complemented one
> another perfectly, and formed an extraordinarily firm rel-
> ationship in which, however faintly, there always lay hidden
> an element of opposition.

About Vernon and Dylan it could be said that their natures
were, under every surface difference, too much alike to
make a firm relationship on both sides; the essential ten-
sion, the hidden 'element of opposition', was lacking.

Most critics, and indeed most people who knew them
both, saw only the differences,—of feeling, behaviour,
attitude, life-style. It was difficult, if not impossible, to
perceive the likeness between two men who, early in their
lives, had found life so strange, so uncontrollable, perhaps
so frightening, that they turned to words instead. The two
men certainly did not perceive this likeness themselves as

they moved towards the beginning of their friendship in 1935; or if they did, it was unconsciously. To the compulsions which gripped them they still, in that early time, gave the name of choice.

CHAPTER THREE: POEMS IN CWMDONKIN DRIVE

The richness of the letters I was now re-reading brought back to me, with the atmosphere of pre-war Swansea and Laugharne, a situation, an era and an excitement which cannot be repeated.—V.W.

Vernon's admiration of his new friend had time to turn into hero-worship in the few weeks after their first meeting before Dylan went to Derbyshire in April to stay with A.J.P. and Margaret Taylor. In Pennard Vernon had read his own poems to Dylan; on the return visit to Cwmdonkin Drive the next week, Dylan read his, from a folder on which he had printed in large capitals the word POEMS. The first poem he read was *Ears in the turrets hear*, and then *Should lanterns shine.* He had completed seven of the sonnets in the sequence *Altar-wise by owl-light in the half-way house,* and these too he read. When he reached the last line of the seventh, "On rose and icicle the ringing handprint", there was a moment of silence, and then he looked up. The lamp behind his head made his golden hair into a halo, and the echo of his beautiful voice still trembled on the air. It was a moment which stayed in Vernon's memory all his life; it was no wonder that the combination of poetry, lamplight and young Adonais not yet dead but already apotheosized, should change Vernon's already heightened feeling into something like adoration. "I was aware", he said, "that I was in the presence of a poet of extraordinary genius". The whole world had shrunk for him to the compass of the small room, and nothing that happened later changed his feelings.

> Praise God, although a time is gone
> That shall not come again,
> If ever morning rightly shone,
> A glass to make all plain,
> The man I mourn can make it live,
> Every fallen grain.

I see the house where we would meet;
I see my steps return;
Kicking the sparks of the Swansea street,
And still those windows burn,
Struck by the sunrise hour of life
With all men's lives to learn.

My echoing footsteps when they stop
Reconstitute the town,
That working window at the top,
The neophyte and clown
Setting the reel and arc-light up
To pull illusion down . . .

Climbing Cwmdonkin's dock-based hill,
I found his lamp-lit room,
The great light in the forehead
Watching the waters' loom,
Compiling there his doomsday book
Or dictionary of doom.

More times than I can call to mind
I heard him reading there.
His eyes with fervour could make blind
All clocks about a stair
On which the assenting foot divined
The void and clustered air.

That was the centre of the world,
That was the hub of time.
The complex vision faded now,
The simple grew sublime.
There seemed no other valid stair
For wondering feet to climb.

That strictest, lie-disrobing act
Testing the poem read
Which, after toil and plumbing,
Left the first cause unsaid,
Showed me his nature then as now,
The life he gave the dead.

There, near Cwmdonkin, first and last,
Witness of lives below,
He held the unrisen wisdom fast
From heaven in overthrow,
Where lamps of hooded meaning cast
Light on the words below.

After he had finished reading the poems, Dylan asked
Vernon if he used a dictionary. Vernon answered that he
occasionally did, but Dylan said, "No, I mean a real dictionary, like this", and took down from a shelf a book
made of folded sheets of brown paper sewn together. It was
a rhyming dictionary, which he had compiled himself, and
to which he constantly made additions. This, he said, was
his Doomsday Book.

He also showed Vernon the manuscript of his story *The
Orchards*. This was written in his minute hand on the
inside of the cover of a large cardboard box made to hold
ladies' blouses. He said that his mother obtained these
boxes for him from an obliging draper, since he found it
helped him to see a story in its entirety rather than on successive pages. He read this story aloud, too; in it appeared
for the first time the name Llareggub, later to become
known all over the world. Dylan told Vernon that it was
from Joyce, the prose-writer he most admired at that time,
that he had learned this kind of word-play. He displayed as
well the manuscripts of *The Lemon* and *A Prospect of the
Sea*, still in the making, and told Vernon about his friend
Tom Warner, to whom the second of these stories was dedicated. Tom was a musician, who had been brought up in
Swansea by two elderly aunts; and once, said Dylan del-
ightedly, when Tom was lying on his bed wondering
anxiously whether he would be able to get a job, and, if
not, whether he would have to play the trumpet for pen-
nies outside the downtown pubs, one of the aunts had
called up to him, "Tom, Tom! *Water the fuchsia!*"

Vernon stumbled down Cwmdonkin Hill to catch the
last bus back to Pennard, dazzled by his new friend's brilliance and exhausted from his day's work in the busy,
understaffed St. Helen's Road branch of Lloyds. He was

not too exhausted, however, even after the half-hour's bus journey, to rush into Wyn Lewis's house and shout, "I have spent the evening with a genius. You must meet him too!"

Wyn's parents' house was next door to the Watkins house, Heatherslade. Wyn and Dylan were born within a month of each other, and both had played in Cwmdonkin Park, members of rival infant gangs: the tots in Wyn's gang were terrorised and rolled in the gravel by the larger, rougher members of the other gang. At this time he was a Cambridge undergraduate, home for the Easter vacation.

Vernon pressed a copy of *18 Poems* on Wyn, and disappeared, as Philip Larkin was to describe him on another occasion, "exalted into the night". There was time before Dylan left for Derbyshire in April for him to come to tea on one more Saturday at Heatherslade; and after tea Vernon took Dylan to Windyridge to meet Wyn and to play croquet.

Wyn and Vernon were fanatical croquet opponents, neither willing to lose, and neither able to believe that if he had lost, it was not merely a fluke which could be easily retrieved in the next game. This meant that the next game had to be played, occasionally until after midnight, with torches and a beady-eyed opponent to hold a handkerchief behind the hoop to make the aperture visible. It was to this serious cut-throat game that Dylan was to be introduced.

Wyn had read *18 Poems* and was prepared to be awed by genius. But Dylan was shy, and at first talked only to Vernon; when he became more at ease, he was neither exhibitionistic nor flamboyant. He talked politely, made the necessary efforts to learn the new game and seemed interested in it. He was courteous and deferential to Wyn's parents. After supper he talked a little about the poetry of W. H. Davies, and read a poem. Apart from the beauty of his voice Wyn could see nothing remarkable about him.

After leaving Derbyshire Dylan went to Ireland, but he was back in Swansea in the autumn, and on the 6th October he sent Richard Church the manuscripts of most of the poems he had written since *18 Poems* (omitting the

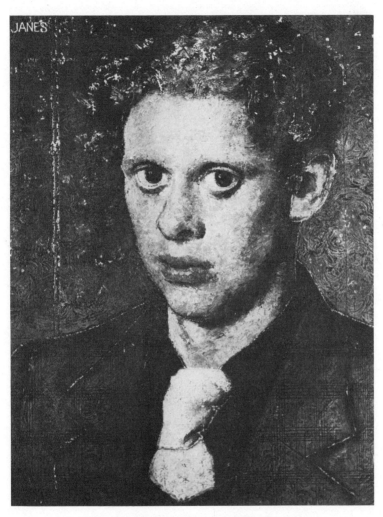

Portrait of Dylan Thomas by Alfred Janes.

(Original in the National Museum of Wales, Cardiff.)

5 Cwmdonkin Drive

'I see the house where we would meet,
I see my steps return,
Kicking the sparks of the Swansea street,
And still those windows burn . . .'

still unfinished sonnet-sequence.) It was now that Vernon
began to see him regularly, as often as two or three
evenings a week. He also went on Wednesdays during his
lunch hour to the Kardomah, where he met Alfred Janes,
Tom Warner, Charles Fisher, John Prichard and other
young men. Dan Jones was abroad by this time, and in fact
Vernon did not meet him until they were both posted to
Bletchley Park during the war. But Dylan talked so much
about him that Vernon, when challenged to give a description of him, was able to do so accurately (much more
accurately, I may say, than if he had observed Dan for himself). For the first time since leaving Repton he was among
men who were interested in and cared about the arts. He
was to remember the Kardomah with affection long after it
had been destroyed in the blitz on Swansea:

> Nobody has rebuilt the Kardomah, where Swansea's rich art-
> ists and poverty-stricken business-men used to meet, on sep-
> arate floors, to discuss shares and pictures. The old shopping
> centre of Swansea is a ruin, as big as the Colosseum; . . . I
> begin to think that Swansea was once a better place.

He grew very fond of Tom Warner and Fred Janes, and
delighted to tell how Fred, when his paintings were being
praised, had noticed that the attractive girl at the next
table appeared to be listening, and whispered, ''More of
that, AND LOUDER!'' Or how, when other artists' work
was discussed and he had waited in vain for a mention of
his own name, he had got up from the table, stared for a
long time into a mirror on the wall, and then sat down
again saying sadly, *''And handsome, too!''*
Delightful though the Kardomah meetings were, they
were not as important to Vernon as the evenings he and
Dylan spent in Cwmdonkin Drive discussing and sometimes revising the poems to go into Dylan's next book.
Church was dubious about their obscurity and their Sur-
realistic content. Vernon and Dylan were indignant at this
unwarranted assumption: Vernon was later to point out
that, although there was Surrealist imagery in the early
stories, the only image in the whole of Dylan's poetry that

could be called Surrealist was in *After the Funeral*, the image of the slit throat of the boy shedding dry leaves.

About Church's accusation of obscurity Dylan cared little. Vernon tried to persuade him to leave out of the book two of the poems, *Now say nay*, and *How Soon the Servant Sun*, which he was sure the critics would attack because of their baffling and provocative confusion of meanings. "Oh, give them a bone", said Dylan carelessly, and added that, as far as he knew, one at least of those poems had "no meaning whatsoever".

Vernon did, however, persuade Dylan to include one very well-known poem, *And Death Shall Have No Dominion*. Dylan was not satisfied with it, and had determined to leave it out. But Vernon, after hearing it read aloud again and again, became excited by what he called its 'impulsive rhythm', and began the routine he and Dylan had devised for the revision of poems. This consisted of reading each line of the poem separately and considering whether there was any word which was not completely satisfactory. If there was, they would hurl words at each other, perhaps forty or fifty possible words which would then be tried in the line. If one of these was accepted, this might change the balance or texture, so that other changes would have to be made. It was an exhaustive and exhausting procedure; but at the end of the evening Dylan had made several changes and had agreed that the poem should now be included in the new book. (I wonder how many lovers of Dylan's poetry, listening to the windy bombastics of this particular poem booming out on memorial occasions, have, like myself, regretted this decision.)

A change which was certainly for the better was also due to Vernon. The last two lines of the poem *Should Lanterns Shine*, on its appearance in *New Verse* in December 1935, were

> Regard the moon, it hangs above the lawn;
> Regard the lawn, it lies beneath the moon.

These lines seem to have no connection with the rest of

the poem, and are, besides, much more like Eliot than Dylan Thomas. The two previous lines,

> The ball I threw while playing in the park
> Has not yet reached the ground

make a much better ending.

All things considered, Dylan was pleased with the poems. He thought them better than the *18 Poems*. They did indeed show a much greater variety of rhythm and stanza form; and even when he felt one of them, such as *I in my Intricate Image* to be not entirely successful, he still thought it to be better than anything he had done up to that time. (He was disappointed that Vernon, on hearing this poem for the first time, did not notice the seventy-two concealed rhyme endings on the letter L.)

Vernon's only criticism of the twenty-five poems was that the lines were too packed with meaning, that there were no 'numb' words and lines to give the poems natural extension. He quoted lines of Yeats in which at least half the words were 'numb':

> But he calls down a blessing on the blossom of the may,
> Because it comes in beauty, and in beauty blows away.

But that was not Dylan's way. "If my readers want a breather, they won't get one from me", he said magnificently. "Let them go away and have a game of table-tennis; then they can come back to my next line."

A poem that Vernon particularly admired was *Then Was My Neophyte*, which was finished about this time. After Dylan died, Vernon often used it in his many readings of Dylan's verse, because he saw it as

> a prophecy of his own melodramatic death,
> shown to him on a film which he as a child,
> whose character has not been formed, sees
> unwinding and projected on a screen . . . under water.

Vernon was not much of a film-goer, even in the thirties, the great days of the film. One reason for this was that he was completely incapable of following a plot. Kingsley Amis said of him that, when he saw the hero of a film pacing up and down in a hospital waiting-room, lighting cigarette after cigarette, his sole deduction was that the chap was a heavy smoker. Dylan loved films; he once told Vernon that he especially enjoyed really bad films, because they gave him a peculiar kind of thrill. His own film-scripts, and his unfinished novel *Adventures in the Skin Trade*, were to show perhaps that he was not capable of inventing sustained narrative; but he could follow a plot. After the selection of *25 Poems* was complete, some of the evenings in Cwmdonkin Drive were spent in reading prose.

Where poetry was concerned Vernon knew as much as, if not more than, Dylan; but his knowledge of prose literature was minimal. Indeed, he believed that reading prose spoiled the ear for poetry, as playing lawn-tennis spoils the hand and eye for rackets. Perhaps he thought prose merely a kind of spoiled poetry; at all events he read nothing but the Bible (mainly the poetic books Job and Ruth, though he knew Isaiah quite well too), the prose of Yeats, which he considered a kind of poetry, and Kierkegaard, whom he considered a kind of poet who happened to write prose.

Dylan, on the other hand, was a voracious reader of prose. He had read Dickens and Joyce at one end of the scale, and every thriller he could lay his hands on at the other. It is no wonder that to Vernon he seemed "fabulously well-read".

This was not D. J. Thomas's opinion. He complained to Vernon one day at supper that his son was terribly narrow in his reading. "Narrow!" said Dylan. "Narrow? Why, *he* stops reading when the words go on to the end of the page."

Not even Dylan could persuade Vernon to go on reading when the lines went on to the end of the page, but he could, and did, read aloud to him. He read Joyce's *Dubliners*, almost his Bible at that time, Djuna Barnes's *Nightwood*, and Caradoc Evans's short stories, doing all the characters, like Sloppy with the Police-news, "in different voices". This was a revelation to Vernon, who, besides being poor at plots, had never really made much of dialogue either. He was amazed, too, to see how Dylan's "jackdaw eye" enabled him to pick up from his reading bits and pieces that would later be filled into their proper places in poems.

For instance, the Doctor's cry in *Nightwood*—"I tell you, Madame, if one gave birth to a heart on a plate, it would say 'Love', and twitch like the lopped leg of a frog" —became, in *After the Funeral*,

> The stuffed lung of the fox twitch and cry Love.

And one day, reading, in the intervals of working on a "poem about churches", a cheap thriller which bored him, he was transfixed by the words, "The shadow is dark directly under the candle". This became the line

> There is loud and dark directly under the dumb flame

from the poem in *The Map of Love* beginning

> It is the sinners' dust-tongued bell claps me to churches.

He told Vernon that in one of his poems he was determined to use the line

> See, see where Christ's blood streams in the firmament!

But he did not live long enough to write that poem.

Vernon has paid tribute to what Dylan did for him in these meetings: "he showed me what was fresh in my work, and what was derivative". Vernon had no such service as this to offer Dylan (and indeed whatever Dylan learned from other poets he learned so early that he seemed to be always learning only from himself) but there were small things he could do, bits of bright stuff he could throw into the treasury for the jackdaw mind to pick out later.

Vernon had always been addicted to reading one poet at a time, perhaps for six months or longer; and the poet he had been reading for a long time now was W. B. Yeats,

> whom I regarded then and still regard as the greatest lyric poet of our age. I already in 1935, when I met Dylan Thomas, owed more to Yeats than to any other poet, as he had shown me something which the others had not been able to show: that is, how a lyric poet should grow old. This was certainly something to do with what Yeats himself called 'the greater sincerity of an artist's life'; but this alone would not have explained his extraordinary capacity for self-renewal; as a

poet, he was willing, at any age, to dedicate himself completely to his vision, believing always in its miraculous fruit. It was not so much that Yeats grew old impressively, but that, as he aged, his poems grew better and more astoundingly fresh, 'moving', as he said, 'continually, like Swedenborg's angels, towards the dayspring of their youth'.

Dylan of course knew all the anthology pieces of Yeats—*The Lake Isle of Innisfree, Aedh Wishes for the Cloths of Heaven, No Second Troy*—but of the great books of the thirties he knew nothing. When he heard them, he agreed with Vernon that Yeats was "the greatest by miles". His own favourite poet remained Hardy; here again he knew only selections, and it was Vernon who lent him his own *Collected Poems of Thomas Hardy*, which enraptured him. Vernon remembered him laying his hand on the book and saying solemnly, "There is not a single poem in this book that I wish had not been written". It was not that he did not see the faults in some of the poems, but that he loved the faults too. "I love all Hardy", he said later, "even bad Hardy—no, especially bad Hardy."

Some of Dylan's friends, and many of his critics and admirers, have thought it strange that Hardy should be so much the foremost of all poets for him. I have never thought it strange; the link between them is very clear. Hardy is above all the celebrator of past happiness or past unhappiness, not because the time was happy or unhappy, but because it is *past*. (Is not this why Hardy is *the* poet for Philip Larkin too?) Dylan began to feel the importance of the past at a time when most young men are thinking only of the present or the future. *Fern Hill, In the White Giant's Thigh, In Country Sleep*, are all eminently Hardyesque poems. It is often assumed that because Dylan's language is complex, his thought must be complex too. But this is not so; his thought is often very simple indeed, as simple as the thought in Hardy's narrative poems, though the presentation is lyric rather than narrative. And almost always the theme is the present in the act of becoming the past, or the remembrance of things past. Dylan is the Proust of poetry.

This was one region where Vernon's thought was more robust than Dylan's. For him one day in the past, the Crucifixion, and one day in the future, the Day of Judgment, were more important than all other times. In his early twenties he had felt as Dylan did, but by the time he was twenty-three he knew that never again would he write "a poem dominated by time".

Still, he liked Hardy; some of the poems he loved, and he was happy to listen to Dylan reading them aloud. Dylan's favourite was always *To Lizbie Brown*, but there were many others he liked to read, particularly *An Ancient to Ancients*, to which, he told Vernon, *And Death Shall Have No Dominion* was a distant relation. The Hardy poem that Vernon liked best and loved to hear Dylan read, was *In Death Divided*:

> I shall rot here, with those whom in their day
> You never knew,
> And alien ones who, ere they chilled to clay,
> Met not my view,
> Will in your distant grave-place ever neighbour you.

In this, as in many other ways, Dylan seemed strangely to influence Vernon from beyond the grave. Some of the elegies Vernon wrote for Dylan were (except for their praise of God) more like Hardy than any others he ever wrote; certainly *A True Picture Restored* has elements of Hardy in it, and *The Exacting Ghost* is very like a Hardy poem indeed, with its syntactical complexities making, as T. R. M. Creighton says, "a grammar of grief".

And it was to Hardy that Vernon turned when he heard that Dylan had died in America, before it was known that his body would be brought home to Laugharne. He took down the blue old-fashioned book that Dylan had handled and read from so often, and without opening it he quoted from *In Death Divided*:

> The eternal tie which binds us twain in one
> No eye will see
> Stretching across the miles that sever you from me.

CHAPTER FOUR: DRINK

Brandy and ripe in my bright, bass prime . . .—D.T.

In September 1936, with the publication of *25 Poems*, Dylan became an established poet. When Edith Sitwell reviewed it in the *Sunday Times* in November, he became famous.

The shape-changer confronted his celebrity as he confronted almost everything else—with shyness, with showing-off, with pleasure, with indifference, with confidence. In Vernon's presence the mask was most often one of amused disdain for reviews and reviewers. He displayed dozens of letters, a few from admirers, but many from angry or bewildered readers complaining of the obscurity of *25 Poems*. One in particular, from a member of the Athenaeum, enraged Vernon, because the writer sneered at the meaninglessness of lines and poems which Vernon thought among the most beautiful in the book.

"I shan't answer any of the others", said Dylan, "but I might write to him."

"And explain to the fool what your poems mean?" said Vernon eagerly.

"Oh, no. I shall just say, Dear member of the Athenaeum, Will you meet me on the steps of your club, so that I can knock you down them?"

Vernon himself was proud of Dylan's reputation and indignant at any criticism of the poems; but he might also have felt some envy. Was his refusal to publish also in part a refusal to compete? He had not, in any case, been so adamant about not publishing as he seems to suggest when he says in his introduction to *Letters to Vernon Watkins*, "My efforts to persuade him to use titles were countered by his efforts to persuade me to send a poem to a magazine." He had in fact sent some poems to the *London Mercury*, of which one was published; and four poems had appeared in an anthology of Cambridgeshire and Hertfordshire poetry in 1927. He did not need a great deal of persuasion to allow Dylan to send two of his poems to Keidrych Rhys for the first number of *Wales.*

Birthdays were always important to Dylan. They were, wrote Vernon,

> always for him occasions for reflection—some of his finest poems were suggested by them—and for unstinted celebration . . . The accident that he arrived in America just before his 39th birthday may have assisted that very instinct of generosity which was to prove fatal to him.

On October 27th, 1936, Vernon spent the evening of Dylan's twenty-second birthday with him. They started off with a drink at the Bay View Hotel, then took turns to ride Vernon's bicycle along the Mumbles Road to Oystermouth, ending up at Dylan's favourite pub, the Mermaid. Vernon recorded this occasion in a long poem called *Sailors on the Moving Land* which was published in *Life and Letters Today* in 1949 (although the first of its many drafts is on pre-war paper, and the last is dated 1956—three years after Dylan's death).

The occasion was a comic one, yet the poem is serious. In drunkenness inhibitions disappear; this was the first— and perhaps, the only—time that Vernon was allowed, or allowed himself, to perceive the essential tragedy of Dylan's life, and the hair's breadth by which he himself had avoided a destiny of the same kind.

> Before the safety curtain dropped
> Upon all knowledge, while we stopped
> The edge of distance, by degrees
> October brought no flying grains
> Rustling behind the Mumbles trains
> Passing our faces where time stopped,
> Leaving this music of the tunnelled seas.
>
> Dusk before war, and swallows in their crowd
> Whirl to a pointed cloud.
> Now they are gone. What instinct chooses?
> Faced by the judgment, who is not a cheat?
> What eye now sees, now loses
> His brother's face, a stranger in the street?

They were already tipsy as they threaded their uncertain
way along the narrow Oystermouth pavements, past the
shops still, in those pre-war days, open till nine or ten
o'clock.

'I have a bicycle that is not mine.'
    'The round moon racing through the clouds is fine.'
'I have seen Lamprey's marble crossed by eels.'
    'Must we be mastered by the moving wheels?' . . .

So to the inner smoke, the quarrelling air,
Angry jolting of a chair,
Edge of the darkness' knife, confessions of despair;

The bitter mermaid sang her worst.
Neither throat could slake its thirst.

Tritons of the sea shed tears,
But you, with terror in your head,
Shook philosophy out of your ears,
Snatched a great light, and said:

'I have a cage of darkness, hiding
The great white innocent bird, the albatross,
And where the waters toss,
This way and that way riding
White horses of the cradle or the fosse.
To wordless islands and the One-Eyed Man,
I know the horrible gulf from which we ran.
Speak, if you know the place where speech began.'

When the pub closed, they were turned out into the
street that heaved like the sea under their feet, and started
up the hill past Oystermouth Castle, sometimes taking
turns to push, or lean over, the bicycle, and sometimes dis-
covering that neither of them was pushing it, so that they
had to retrace their steps to find it lying in the gutter.
Once, in the bright moonlight, the shadow of Vernon's
head appeared to have grown horns (in reality the handle-
bars); Dylan became terrified, insisted that he was walking with the Devil, and had with great difficulty to be persuaded to go on.

Time. Time. Time. Time.
Thunderbolts of death and birth.
Thunderbolts of rut and rout.
How many from the contemporary tomb
Who had found warmth and comfort here, stepped out
To the stampeding Earth.

So from Oystermouth's nets of Wales
Followed by the fishes' tails
And every print and spoor of grief,
Where the dull trees were lopped of every leaf
We climbed through darkness where you danced about,
Gay as a babbling thief.

Oystermouth Castle floated round
A sea of undulating ground.
Two moon-flung shadows, bent to steal
The navel-stone no man had found,
Zig-zagged uphill, fell flat across the wheel.

Two with a bicycle, two men with horns.
Two shadowed quarrellers pushing two moons.

It took Vernon three hours to cover the seven miles to
Pennard. He could never remember where Dylan left him;
it was probably at the Murton end of Newton Lane, where
he might have been lucky enough to catch the last bus
back to Swansea. All through the monumental hangover
that followed Vernon could not forget what he had understood for the first time; the profound unhappiness that
lived beneath the clown's mask.

And morning, morning, morning followed fleet;
The playing pavings, gathering flying feet,
Hammered the dark of eyelids closed beneath
                                        their sunny sheet. . .

The lips stammer against the light.
Sleeps holds them, forming the oracle, saying:
'Able to touch'. I woke up, saying,
'I was able to touch his sorrow.'

It was excuse enough in Vernon's mind for any subsequent drunkenness on Dylan's part; *if* he drank too much it was because his suffering was too great to be borne. Usually, however, Vernon discounted stories of Dylan's drunkenness as exaggerations; this was the only time he had seen Dylan drunk, and it was, after all, a birthday celebration.

Wyn Lewis had never seen Dylan drunk, either, and Vernon did not tell him about the October débacle. It was therefore with some confidence that he, at the suggestion of Ian Watt, the Secretary of the Literary Society, invited Dylan to Cambridge to give a talk. Since the publication of *25 Poems* the new and remarkable young poet had been a good deal talked about; the Literary Society felt it an advantage to have a member who had played croquet with him.

Dylan responded amiably but more practically than Wyn had expected; he asked for £5 and his expenses. This was a fairly large amount for an undergraduate society in the thirties, but it was agreed on. The talk was to be a demolition of such contemporary giants as T. S. Eliot, Pound, Auden and Spender.

Neither of Dylan's biographers gives any account of this visit to Cambridge. Constantine FitzGibbon quotes a letter from Dylan to David Higham of February 11th, saying that he will be going to Cambridge on the next day: Paul Ferris refers to a letter to the *T.L.S.* in 1962 by Professor E. M. W. Tillyard, describing Dylan's "feeble, maudlin state of intoxication" in an undergraduate's rooms. A detailed account, given to me by Wyn Lewis, may be of interest here, as showing very clearly Dylan's real fear of public occasions and how this fear influenced his actions and reactions.

Wyn met Dylan at the station in mid-afternoon and took him to his lodgings in Park Parade, where tea and Ian Watt were waiting. But Dylan told Wyn that he had already had thirty pints of beer, and wanted more beer, not tea. Wyn would have been more apprehensive than he was if Dylan had not been so pleasantly mellow, talking of his own poetry and pleased that Wyn knew *25 Poems* (a copy of which had in fact been pressed on him by Vernon soon after its publication.) He played on and with Wyn's piano, achieving something like Debussy's *Clair de Lune* by ear. He ate and drank tea, talked sociably to Patric Dickinson and other undergraduates who came in after tea and expanded pleasurably in their obvious admiration. Wyn and Ian Watt felt that all was going smoothly. It would probably have continued to go smoothly if they could have stayed there until the talk began.

But they had been invited to a sort of cocktail party reception given by a wealthy South African undergraduate, and Dylan had to be half coaxed, half forced to go. He was always terrified of formal occasions, or of occasions which he thought, without reason, might be formal, and his terror, as so often, showed itself as surliness and obstinacy. At last Wyn and Ian Watt, both very tall, took Dylan's small body between them and bore him off.

A hush fell as they entered the South African's plushy rooms. Their host hurried over to them, carrying a tray of glasses full of South African sherry. His shrill and gushing welcome focussed attention on the newcomers, and Dylan had almost to be prevented from backing out of the door. Embarrassed and apprehensive, he downed a glass of sherry (which he hated) in one gulp and, in the ensuing silence, gulped another three in quick succession, crying "More!" between each.

The sherry had an immediate effect. He aggressively demanded whisky. While this was being fetched, the nonplussed host introduced him, by way of distraction, to the belle of the English faculty, a stunning young lady with (unfortunately, as it turned out) a double row of buttons marching from the shoulders of her close-fitting green dress down to strategic points on her figure.

Dylan went immediately into his Harpo Marx act. Eyes bulging, twitching fingers outstretched towards the final buttons, he made ready to pounce. The young lady shrank back dismayed towards the protective frown of a don's wife. Nobody laughed. Dylan, disappointed, seized his glass of whisky and applied himself to it.

The disconcerted Secretary decided that Dylan must be taken away. The undergraduates were embarrassed and the dons and their wives icily unaware. Wyn said nervously that poets had always been a law unto themselves, but only the silence answered him. Only Dylan himself was unaffected; as he was borne away between his two guards, he shouted cheerfully back over his shoulder "Goodbye, everybody, see you later". Then he wrenched himself free and rolled down the stairs.

Picked up and dusted, he was half-led, half-carried along Trinity Street, making obscene gestures and mouthing loud invitations to every passing woman. In the merciful dusk he was at last led into Ian Watt's rooms in Ram Yard, where he immediately stumbled to a couch and fell asleep. Wyn and Ian picked at the delicate crab salad and sipped white wine while their guest snored.

At ten to eight they could wait no longer. A bowl of water and a sponge, liberally applied, resulted in Dylan's sudden awakening in a furious temper. He did not know where he was and when told refused to accept that he had agreed to talk to any kind of society. He staggered to a full-length Victorian mirror and addressed himself in scathing terms—"What do you think you're doing? Who *are* you, eh? You tell the world who you are"—while the waiting taxi ticked up the minutes.

At last the two undergraduates became desperate and almost manhandled their captive poet into the taxi. He was bitterly offended, but, once in the taxi, began to comb his hair and straighten his tie and feel for his notes. (The dinner-jacket borrowed for this very occasion from Tom Warner was doubtless stuffed into his suitcase and utterly forgotten.)

Wyn and Ian Watt urged the taxi on, spurred by the thought of all those people who had been so indignant at the sherry party growing even more indignant as they waited. It was already fifteen minutes later than the advertised time of the talk. At St. John's they hurried Dylan along the corridors, Wyn hastily composing some sort of apology. But in the lecture-room there was almost no-one to apologise to. Six students sat among a wilderness of chairs.

One of them told Wyn in whispers that all the dons and their wives at the party had decided to boycott the talk and had advised the undergraduates to do the same. Wyn and Ian, after a hasty consultation, left Dylan in charge of the audience—or the audience in charge of Dylan—and rushed out, one into the college, one into the street, where like the servants at the wedding-feast, they ''gathered together all as many as they found, both bad and good''.

By half past eight, a couple of dozen undergraduates had joined the original six. Dylan, asking peevishly, ''Shall we start now?'' slapped his thick script (about twenty pages covered in his neat miniscule handwriting) on the reading-desk, leaned over it and began muttering. For the first two or three minutes what was not inaudible sounded like gibberish. The wretched organisers sweated where they sat. But gradually a phrase or two, then a sentence, began to come clear, of such riveting quality that the audience sat up as though electrified.

Gradually Dylan got into his stride. For more than an hour he gave a pyrotechnical display of wild, brilliant, anarchic comments on the contemporary literary scene. Attracted by the shrieks of laughter, other people looked round the door, listened a moment and sidled in. Long before the end of the talk the room was crowded and people were standing in the corridor. When Dylan finally came to a stop, tremendous cheering and applause broke out, the audience crowded round him, and he was borne off to the rooms of Wyn's tutor, where he sat by the fire for hours, drinking coffee and telling Welsh stories to a fascinated and ever-growing crowd. It was a triumph snatched from the jaws of disaster, anticipating by twenty years similar evenings that were to take place in colleges all over America. Both Wyn and Dylan were euphoric as they trailed away to bed in the small hours of the morning, although Dylan was slightly oppressed at being left alone in the grand and rather sombre guest-room.

He was due to return to London the next morning, and

Wyn arrived at about nine o'clock to take him to the station. A gyp had brought him breakfast, but he was still in bed, bleary, sullen, and coughing appallingly.

"Did they bring you a nice breakfast?" said Wyn politely.

Dylan's voice was intensely bitter. "Oh, yes, if you call about a pint of blood in your porridge *nice*"; and after another frightful explosion of coughing he held out to Wyn his bloodstained handkerchief.

Wyn was horrified. Was Dylan having a haemorrhage? Would he die in the guest-room? Was it because of his efforts the night before? Ought he to have a doctor or be rushed to hospital? He was half-apprehensive, half-relieved when Dylan grumblingly got up and dressed, but refused to be taken to the station on the grounds that he had accepted an invitation to lunch—where, he did not say. He disappeared shortly after, and Wyn lost track of him completely. Occasionally during the following week they ran into each other, in the streets, in Sydney Sussex, in King's, in Magdalene; Dylan was enjoying himself tremendously, feted, lionised, floating from college to college on a wave of adulation. His suitcase remained unopened in Wyn's rooms. One day it was not there.

It may be pertinent, in a chapter largely about drinking, to give my own interpretation of Dylan's need for alcohol. It seemed to me that in this area too the split in his personality showed clearly. The poet drank very little, and needed to drink not at all; writing, reading or talking about poetry, he could make do with a glass of water if nothing else was to be had. The child, on the other hand, needed constant oral gratification; sweets or pop would do as well as beer. If he was at ease in his company, liked and admired (not flattered), he rarely seemed to drink to excess, and certainly he never showed in these circumstances the uneasy urgency of the true alcoholic for more and stronger drink. I remember him spending a whole evening with Vernon and Alfred Janes, reading and discussing the first draft of his Bank Holiday script, on a single bottle of beer. But any pressure, any anxiety, any uncertainty—and res-

pites from all of these were rare in Dylan's life—drove him
to alcohol as a child turns to its mother's breast for comfort.

CHAPTER FIVE: THE END OF AN ERA

There still lives the memory of those bygone years filled with warmth and laughter, a delicate sense of what was frail and yet unperishable in our adventure through life.—F.D-L.

In the autumn term of 1936 a young French *assistant* at the Swansea Grammar School was asked by D. J. Thomas, Dylan's father, to contribute a short article to the school magazine. Francis Dufau-Labeyrie was a Gascon from Dax, tall, dark, dark-eyed, perhaps something of a Don Juan. He was a student at the Sorbonne, studying for the 'agrégation' and complying with requirements by writing a thesis on Ernest Dowson. He gave conversation classes to the Grammar School boys, for which he received £10 a month.

His article was accepted by D. J. Thomas, who suggested that he should meet Dylan, since they were both interested in English poetry. "My son . . . wants to become the poet-laureate, or something like that." Francis turned up one day at the Kardomah, early in 1937, and became for a short time, until Dylan left Swansea in April, his drinking-companion. For some reason Dylan was at this time attracted by the dockland area, where he and Francis would roam about in the dark, dropping in at small pubs, and usually finishing up at the Metropole Hotel near the station, where both were drawn to the barmaid, a sumpt-uously-endowed young lady called Vera. Francis recalls that one evening he had been invited to dinner at Cwm-donkin Drive. He and Dylan had a pre-dinner drink which unfortunately went on until closing-time. Remorseful, nervous, and quite drunk, they hurried too late up the hill, to be met by Mrs. Thomas's anxious and offended rebukes. The elaborate dinner she had prepared was still being kept warm, although D.J. had gone to bed in disgust. "Great was my embarrassment", Francis recalls, "and so was Dylan's. We apologised, and I remember how touching he was in his affectionate acceptance of his mother's scolding."

48

Francis Dufau-Labeyrie
In Ireland, on the visit to W. B. Yeats, Summer 1938.

Francis had been all this time gradually becoming a closer friend of Vernon's mainly because of Vernon's great interest in French verse.

Vernon soon invited me to meet his mother and father, with whom he lived in their lovely 'Heatherslade' home, on top of the Pennard cliffs. One Sunday morning in February or March, I set out by bus from Swansea. It snowed, and it snowed, and it snowed, as Dylan later wrote in *A Christmas in Wales*, and the bus, a red double-decker affair transporting me as sole passenger, could not go beyond Bishopston. I got out there and trudged the rest of the long way, with the wind in my face, ankle-deep in snow, to 'Heatherslade' . . . I clearly remember my hand on the latch, the click I still hear, distinctly, as I pushed the low gate against the thick layer of snow behind it.

Vernon commemorated this first meeting in his poem *The Fire in the Snow:*

> Come in. The brilliant, beautiful
> Sun has dropped, and the noon-cracked pool
> Freezes back. Come, seek from night
> Gloom's fire, where the unlit room is white.
>
> I wait, intent, by the firelit stones
> Strewn with chopped wood and fallen cones.
> Come in, and watch with me in dark
> The red spark eating the black bark.
>
> Bright, from fields where the snow lies thick,
> From sunk fields to the latch's click
> You come; and your eyes, most watchful, glow,
> Seeing in the firelight the brightness of snow.

Francis had lodgings at 11, Calvert Terrace with a Mrs. James, an unusually tolerant landlady, who would pour out the tea for her lodger and his friends. She also allowed him to give parties, at one of which Dylan attempted to shampoo the carpet with beer. Francis left Swansea in July 1937, to spend the summer vacation in France, just before the momentous news of Dylan's marriage reached Vernon.

Dylan's letter announcing the marriage was characteristic of him: the news comes only after an apology for altering one of Vernon's poems, and a discussion of the first
number of *Wales*, a new magazine edited by Keidrych
Rhys. Dylan had ever since he met Vernon tried to persuade him to send his poems to some magazine for publication: he felt that there was an element of cowardice in an
artist who refused to submit his work to public scrutiny.
Keidrych Rhys had asked Dylan to look out for contrib-
utions for his first issue, and Dylan had picked up at
Heatherslade two poems, *Griefs of the Sea* and *Old Triton
Time.*

Vernon's pleasure at seeing his poems in print quickly
changed to rage as he saw that *Griefs of the Sea* had been
altered, and that the nature of the changes made it clear
that Dylan was responsible.

> We had always agreed to suggest any improvement to each
> other in a poem where it seemed to go wrong, and in this part-
> icular poem Dylan had persuaded me to make one change of a
> word, but to alter a poem without the other's consent was to
> me unthinkable.

Furiously and in secret Vernon spent all his lunch-hours
and the next Saturday afternoon after the publication of
Wales making the necessary alterations in every copy of
Wales in every bookshop in Swansea. He wrote to Dylan a
letter full of curses, beginning, ''This is just to wish you an
extra sweat in your worst nightmare.''

Dylan apologised for the ''Thowdlerised'' poem, giving
an explanation for the changes which was almost certainly
untrue. Only in the third paragraph of his letter did he tell
Vernon about his marriage. It was not long before he
brought Caitlin to the little house in Bishopston where his
parents now lived. On 30th August Vernon wrote to
Francis about his first meeting with her:

> Dylan came home with his wife Caitlin ('Caitlin ni
> Houlihan') last week, and the first day he was home they
> came over here to supper. She is a beautiful and very nice girl,
> with wonderful gold hair like the incarnation of light, and

still blue eyes like flowers. When she smokes a cigarette she looks very like Dylan and her remarks are like his, but softer, and in a lower key.

Men, when their great friends marry, are often uneasy and mistrustful that their intimacy will wither away because of the new wife. If Vernon felt this at all, he never showed it. Caitlin simply became a part of the romantic aura in which Dylan lived in Vernon's mind. Passionate love merely completed the picture—that Orpheus should find, not lose, his Eurydice, and live happily ever after in a world of pure poetry.

Caitlin's beauty made her the perfect wife for a poet. In photographs she looks pretty, elegant, handsome; but no photograph shows the loveliness of her colouring. Her hair really was 'wonderful'; in sunlight or firelight it blazed with red-gold brilliance, her eyes were cornflower-blue, and her complexion was as Yeats described Maud Gonne's, "like light falling through the apple blossom." Dylan is said to have spoken before his death of his wife's radiance, of the 'illumination' about her. Certainly I have seen her hair appear incandescent, as though it were actually shooting off sparkling rays into the air around her as she shook her head. Dylan said to Vernon once, after Llewelyn was born, as they watched her feeding her child, "What I love about Caitlin is that she changes all the time. One day she will look quite plain, then she will be so beautiful that you can't look at her without being struck blind."

Vernon himself found her beauty remarkable, and commemorated it in several poems. "That golden wife", he called her in one. She had entered the charmed circle in which Dylan lived, and was thereafter to be immune from criticism, as he was. However outrageous her behaviour in later years, Vernon accepted it. Only once, when she was dissatisfied with a performance of *The Marriage of Figaro*, saying savagely, "Oh, if even Mozart lets you down . . ." was he slightly deprecatory. He would never take sides with one or the other in their frequent quarrels, and indeed preferred to think that the quarrels were a mere facade.

Caitlin and Dylan at Heatherslade, July 1938.
'. . . Beethoven accompanied our croquet . . .'

Perhaps they sometimes were. One night when they had been quarrelling violently and unpleasantly in the pub, so that even Vernon began to feel anxious, they fell into each other's arms as soon as the front door of Sea View shut behind them, giggling and congratulating each other on the tremendous show they had put up for the audience in the bar.

But the quarrels came later. Wyn Lewis remembers Caitlin in the first months of her marriage as being quiet, almost withdrawn, enigmatically silent among the talkers, totally absorbed by Dylan; attentive to every word and movement of his, seeming to be completely devoted to him. The photograph of her opposite page 179 of Fitz-Gibbon's *Life* expresses this very well: as oblivious of the camera as of the hole in her jersey, she rests her head against Dylan's breast, a look of dreamy happiness on her beautiful face.

Her devotion to and absorption in Dylan were so like Vernon's own that he felt no jealousy of the marriage. It has been suggested by both FitzGibbon ("aethereal . . . other-worldly . . . his gossamer-like personality . . .") and Ferris (". . . gentle, even-tempered . . .") that Vernon was constitutionally sweet-natured and that it was therefore easy for him to put up with Dylan's vagaries and to tolerate his weaknesses. But this was not the case. Vernon's standards for his family and other friends were exacting, and he could be harshly outspoken if they were not adhered to: at Bletchley Park he once put up on the public notice-board a large printed announcement that a certain Flight-Sergeant had not repaid a debt. When his outraged colleague shouted that he would sue for defamation of character, Vernon responded immediately, "If you've got the money for that, you can pay me what you owe me—and right here!" He got his money back. On another occasion the whole of the female staff at Lloyds Bank was in tears because, being in charge of the Post, he would not let one girl catch her bus until she had accounted for the deficit of a 1½d stamp.

It is true that his manner could be—and often was—

what my father affectionately used to call "half-soaked",
and what one of his colleagues at Bletchley referred to as
"safe in the arms of Jesus". But this vague, dreamy court-
esy was merely a film with which he economically protected his real personality. In matters which did not interest him—that is, in nine-tenths of the ordinary affairs of
living—he could play the Absent-minded Poet to such perfection that the role took him over, and he was more
absent than he wished to be; but when his own or others'
rights were infringed, or when art was insulted, or sometimes when (it must be admitted) he did not get his own
way, he could be aggressive, domineering, even downright
rude. I have seen him in a rage so great that his face was the
colour of wood-ash, and I have seen colleagues or neigh-
bours aghast at the appearance of this fiery persona.

He could be infinitely patient over poetry, waiting years
for a line to work itself out; in all other ways he was extremely impatient. He would always prefer to walk rather
than wait a few moments for a bus; on one occasion he
bodily up-ended a grandfather clock which refused to go,
and on another he battered into a sheet of metal an oil-
stove whose wick he could not turn down. Verbally too he
could be unexpectedly aggressive: he did not get a commission in the R.A.F. because of his scathing attack, in his
OCTU interview, on a Wing-Commander who questioned
him (as he thought, not seriously) on his recently-published
book of poems. When he left the RAF police he told their
Warrant-Officer and Flight-Sergeants (he was himself only
a corporal at the time) that he never expected to meet "a
bigger bunch of crooks" anywhere.

So, if Dylan could get away with anything where Vernon
was concerned, it was not because Vernon was particularly
patient or gentle; if he could do no wrong in Vernon's eyes
it was because he was unique. Vernon might be moment-
arily angry with him, when he altered the poems, or, later,
when he did not turn up at Vernon's wedding: but one
word from Dylan would defuse the anger and bring back
the old devotion, even if the word was patently untrue.

After their visit to Bishopston, when they saw Vernon

several times, and Caitlin was initiated into croquet, Dylan and Caitlin stayed with Caitlin's mother in Hampshire until the spring of 1938. Vernon sent them a jack-in-the-box for Christmas; Dylan, thanking him for the present in February, sent a photograph of himself:

> It's one of many: this is the toughest. Why I want you to think of me,—photographically, when I'm not about—as a tough, I don't know. Anyway, it's very big; you can write a poem on the back, draw whiskers on it, or advertize Kensitas in the front window.

The photograph, carelessly stuck in a thin envelope, arrived bent down its length. Dylan did look tough, like a handsome young gangster lighting the last cigarette in a dark doorway before moving in for the kill. And Vernon did write a poem (though not on its back) in which he tried to resolve some of the contradictions he felt to be inherent not only in Dylan's nature but in their friendship. He called it *Portrait of a Friend.*

> He has sent me this
> Late and early page
> Caught in the emphasis
> Of last night's cartonnage,
> Crumpled in the post,
> Bringing to lamplight
> Breath's abatement,
> Over-and-under-statement,
> Mute as a mummy's pamphlet
> Long cherished by a ghost.
>
> Who for annunciation has
> The white wings of the sheldrake,
> Labouring water's praise,
> The blind shriek of the mandrake,
> Broken shells for story,
> Torn earth for love's near head
> Raised from time's estuary,
> Fed by the raven's bread;
> A trespasser in tombs,
> He bids the grey dust fall,
> Groans in the shaping limbs:
> 'All stars are in my shawl.'

Who feels the deathbound sighs,
Mocks the Winged Horse's fake,
Toiling, as with closed eyes,
Love's language to remake,
To draw from their dumb wall
The saints to a worldly brothel
That a sinner's tongue may toll
And call the place Bethel.

Trusting a creaking house
His roof is ruinous,
So mortal. A real wind
Beats on this house of sand
Two tides like ages buffet.
The superhuman, crowned
Saints must enter this drowned
Tide-race of the mind
To guess or understand
The face of this cracked prophet,
Which from its patient pall
I slowly take,
Drop the envelope,
Compel his disturbing shape,
And write these words on a wall
Maybe for a third man's sake.

(Dylan is said by Constantine FitzGibbon to have read this poem aloud in the spring of 1944, and, on closing the book, to have remarked, "in an entirely matter-of-fact tone of voice" to his future biographer, "And of course the third man, Constantine, is you.")

While Dylan was in Hampshire, he kept up a fairly regular correspondence with Vernon. Each sent poems of his own and criticised the other's poems. Dylan called his long poems 'exhausters'; Vernon preferred to call a long poem an 'opus', which naturally made the short ones into 'opossums'. Dylan sent "my sixty-line year's work", which turned out to be the poem to Caitlin, *I make this in a warring absence*, and "one I have spent a great deal of time on", which was the first part of *In Memory of Ann Jones*, both afterwards to become anthology pieces. Vernon was to write afterwards of the excitement with which he first saw these poems.

Still, he was glad when Dylan came back to Bishopston in early April, 1938. In his edition of the *Letters*, Vernon says that Dylan spent three months staying with his parents; it was in fact less than two, since on the 9th May Vernon wrote to Francis describing his first visit to their new home in Gosport Street, Laugharne, saying that before they went away he had been seeing a great deal of them, "every other day".

Caitlin especially would have been glad to get away from the home of her parents-in-law, to Heatherslade, where she could sun-bathe, walk on the cliffs, run down to any of the bays within half-a-mile of the house to swim—always her great passion—and, in the evenings, listen silently to Dylan and Vernon reading poetry, play croquet, or, sometimes, Lexicon, that pleasant fore-runner of Scrabble at which she was almost always beaten by the others. But once, when Vernon's parents were playing too, her face lit up and she prepared to lay down a whole word. Dylan, curious, looked over her arm, and immediately put his hand over her cards. "No, Cat, no", he said, his face a mixture of amusement and consternation, "no, really, you can't put that down."

"Can't put it down!" she expostulated, "Why, ING gets eight points and K is another six!" Although she was finally persuaded not to play her hand, she evidently found Dylan's veto quite inexplicable and at last assumed that it must be an attempt to prevent her winning. Nothing could show more clearly the chasm between Dylan's background and Caitlin's.

Either the young couple had been given some house-warming presents or Dylan for once had some money in the first Gosport weeks. Vernon wrote to Francis, "I brought small provisions like tinned fruit from Carmarthen market but they already had a lot." But it can only have been from motives of economy that Dylan for a short time gave up smoking cigarettes. "He and Caitlin both smoke a pipe", wrote Vernon, "—often sharing one.'' (This economy drive was still on in an even severer stage, on the 16th June, when Dylan wrote to Henry Treece, ''I haven't a single penny, a half-penny, or filed French slot-coin . . . Bitter, cruel Laugharne; my pipe is full of butt-ends from the grate . . .'')

It was Richard Hughes, author of the best-seller, *High Wind in Jamaica*, who had found the little house in Gosport Street for Dylan and Caitlin. Dylan wrote rather misleadingly to Treece, ''The village also contains bearded Richard High-Wind Hughes, but we move, in five hundred yards, in two or more different worlds: he owns the local castle, no roof and all, and lives in a grand mansion by its side and has a palace in Morocco.'' The words were misleading, because they implied that the two worlds were separate; whereas Richard Hughes regularly invited the young couple to lunch or dinner, gave them money, and, in 1941, invited them to stay at the Castle while he served in the Navy.

Vernon met him for the first time on his May visit to Laugharne. He described the meeting in a letter to Francis,

> . . . in walked Richard Hughes like a very rich, bearded telegraph-post. Electric messages of an avuncular kind trickled from his beard as he stood quite still, never looking at me but straight ahead of him as if a spider were hanging half-way between him and the person he was talking to. He was nice but I was glad when he went . . . Dylan says his wife is so rich she can't hold her eyelids up . . .

Vernon was later to enlarge his account of this interview for his foreword to *A High Wind in Jamaica*:

> The sun now lit up the newly-painted room where we had breakfast, and we had just finished when there were two knocks on the door. ''That will be Hughes'', said Dylan. This visitation gave the surname an accent of awe.
> If the awe of expectation was considerable, the awe of the presence was much greater. I saw in the doorway a figure tall and solemn, with a high, white forehead and black, curly beard, his powerful hands resting on a strong cane. On this he leaned in order not to dwarf still further the low doorway on whose threshold he stood. I was quickly introduced, and he

moved with an evenness of step and intonation into the
room, rising there almost to the raftered ceiling, and then
standing stock still opposite the window, black-bearded and
impressive, like a sea captain who had taken up a vantage
point in a small boat, focussing, with an invisible telescope,
on something none of us could see. His eye travelled from the
white rafters round the walls of the room to the floor, and
ours followed his until all our heads were inclined down. ''I
like your lilac-coloured beams'', he said. Our eyes shot up in-
credulously to the roof that had seemed white. While he, too,
studied them he murmured without changing his posture:
''And I like the feet of your table''.

In June Vernon and Francis went to Ireland to visit W. B.
Yeats. That visit, long looked-forward-to, has been well-
documented elsewhere, and is in any case commemorated
in Vernon's long poem *Yeats in Dublin.* On the way back,
cycling from Fishguard to Laugharne ''on saddles that
bruised us unmercifully'', they spent two days with Dylan
and Caitlin:

> When I stayed with Dylan Thomas in Laugharne on my way
> back from seeing Yeats in Dublin in the summer of 1938 I was
> struck by the difference between them. Both were men of
> undoubted genius, but whereas Yeats spoke like a musically
> controlled oracle, Dylan Thomas, with his abundant imagin-
> ation and quick intelligence was prepared to challenge
> everything he said. Not that Dylan Thomas did not admire
> Yeats' poetry immensely, because he did. But he distrusted,
> at the age of twenty-three, pontifical statements, or state-
> ments that sounded pontifical. Yeats had told me: 'There
> must always be a quality of nonchalance in a poet's work.'
> Dylan would not accept this. And Yeats had added: 'The
> young poets toil too much.'—'He should come *here*', Dylan
> said.

Anarchy and iconoclasm was one thing: Vernon had
himself been anarchic at Repton, and rather enjoyed
knocking down images. But where Yeats was the eikon to
be destroyed, it was a different thing. From no-one but
Dylan would such heresy be accepted. It was a measure of
Vernon's feeling for Dylan. The following Christmas
the party at Heatherslade played Towers, ''an absurd and

most embarrassing game,'' in which the player and two other named persons are on top of a tower on which there is only room for two; the player must choose which of the two is to be pushed over the edge, giving his reasons. ''Fig* put a dreadful one to me'', Vernon confessed to Francis, ''He said: 'If you were on top of a tower with Yeats and Francis . . . I can only say that Yeats is still there . . .'' If the two on the tower had been Yeats and Dylan, it is certain that Vernon would have pitched himself over without a moment's hesitation.

In July Dylan and Caitlin moved from Gosport Street to a larger house, Sea View. The weekend before they moved was spent in Bishopston, almost certainly to beg, borrow or steal some household equipment for their new six-roomed mansion. On the Saturday night Vernon's mother took them all to the theatre to see a Noel Coward play. Vernon reported to Francis that Dylan ''said he was sorry they had to rush back to Laugharne so quickly, that after 'sweet aloes' they had left with 'bitter goodbyes'''.

Vernon admired the ''huge new four-storey house, which is like a house in a fairy-tale and is one. The basement'', he told Francis,

> has hooks on the ceiling and we hung on one of them a slab of meat which I'd bought for them in Carmarthen market. *You* would make short work of it but it would last them, perhaps, 4 days. We couldn't hang the cheese.

Early in September a memorable visit took place, which Dylan still remembered two years later. ''I didn't tell you'', Vernon wrote to Francis,

> that we all went down there to see them . . . a fortnight ago—in Wyn Lewis's car. Wyn wasn't there, but David Lewis drove . . . We all went down to Pendine sands where everyone in turn . . . drove the car. I was the only one who, after at least twenty attempts, failed to start. Even Dylan succeeded, with the throttle full out managed to do 10 miles an hour—in soft sand. Then everyone had to get out and heave the car out of it. Caitlin drove well, so did David's friend, and I grew very

*Vernon's great friend Eric Falk. They had been at Repton together.

jealous and pleaded for one more try. I had it, and when I sailed past Dot [his sister] and Fig at 50 miles an hour Fig's only comment to Dot was 'This is the end'.

The extent to which Vernon was prepared to go merely to hear Dylan read two short poems is shown by an incident recounted in a letter to Francis in the autumn of 1938. "We went to a concert in the Brangwyn Hall . . . in full evening dress . . . After the concert we took a bus to Mrs. James's [Francis' former landlady], broke in on her and without overture or explanation switched on the wireless—Why?—For Dylan's broadcast.—Missed the last bus —got home by taxi."

Francis was now an assistant teacher at the Beckenham and Penge County School for boys. His landlady was very different from Mrs. James: she had platinum hair and a shapely figure. Francis told Vernon with some embarrassment that one of his friends, calling to see him and being told, "Mr. Labeyrie isn't here; he comes and goes, you know", had said with an admiring look, "I expect he comes more often than he goes." He had in common with Vernon and Dylan a passionate and amused interest in words; he and Vernon continually engaged in word-play and exchanged taunts. "You can have the stone you threw at 'Yeats' Tower' back with a year's moss on it", wrote Vernon. "If I were talking to you you would, in your quite intolerable way, work in a proverb about the stone rolling, and get it wrong, as usual—a rolling stone gathers most noise, or something of the sort."

But Francis' grasp of the nuances of colloquial English continually improved (in a letter from Beckenham he wrote, "Your idea of going to Chatham [for conversation] is very acceptable but why not take a few books with us and meet at Reading? or shall I wheel you in a pram up to Motherwell? or else we could absorb a comfortable quantity of bile beans and suddenly wake up for a meeting in Liverpool?") He was fascinated by Dylan's work, and in 1937 had completed his first translation of the short story *A Prospect of the Sea*, which he had read in the spring issue of *Life and Letters Today*. Vernon helped with explanations and suggestions, and the first version was shown to Dylan, who, though his knowledge of French was rudimentary, listened with interest and helped to insure that the translation was as accurate as possible in the rendering of fine shades of meaning. José Corti, a well-known Parisian publisher who had made a name by promoting the then avant-garde French writers (including the surrealists) was very much interested in *Perspective sur la Mer*, but, since Dylan was then completely unknown in France, could not publish it in "plaquette" form without some preliminary funding. In the event, it was published in the 1946 August-September issue of *L'Arche*, an advanced literary review edited by Jean Anvrouche and Dominique Aury.

Francis also translated *The Orchards* and *The Map of Love*, and after the war was to translate the whole of *Portrait of the Artist as a Young Dog*. He wrote to Vernon in March 1938:

> I have had a terrible dream about Dylan. I dreamed he was drowned in the sea he had described in one of his stories. I could see the front page of the book, with a huge sail-ship drawn on it being tossed on a raging sea. In the corner, under the waves, there was Dylan's face. But I mustn't tell you how it was, the sun and sky are too beautiful today, and Dylan is terribly nice.

But although 1938 was the year of Munich, and it became obvious that war was sooner or later inevitable, Dylan himself had no dreams of disaster. Vernon said that it seemed to him in retrospect that Dylan was happier at Sea View than he would ever be again. The perpetual money worries never seemed to be in evidence when Vernon went to Laugharne or Dylan came to Bishopston or, if they occasionally were, Vernon could produce pleasure with gifts of money, food or drink. Any quarrels were still lovers' quarrels. Vernon offered to help clear the table once at Sea View, to be told magnificently, "The woman does all that. *We* must get on with our poems." Caitlin was not always so complaisant, though: once Vernon took a bag of ripe plums as a gift, and Dylan, lying luxuriously on the sofa, asked for one. Caitlin snatched the bag from under Vernon's outstretched hand. "No", she snapped. "He has to get up and fetch a plum if he wants one". There was a silence, broken at last by a soft wheedling voice from the sofa. "Ca-at. Can I have a plum?"

Absolute silence.

"Ca-at. Can I have a plum—just one?"

Silence.

"Ca-at", very plaintively, "can I have a plum—a very little one?"

Still in fierce silence, Caitlin turned on her way out to the kitchen, with the bag still in her hand, and bombarded him savagely with every plum in the bag.

Dylan lay quite still with his eyes closed until the rain of fruit had stopped, then philosophically picking up a plum which had fallen on his lap—"Right", he said, "now we can get on with our poems."

The poems they were getting on with that summer and autumn were revisions of *Portrait of a Friend*, *The Collier*, *Call it all Names*, and a translation of Novalis' hymn *Wenn Alle Untreu Werden* ("That hymn must be great in the original", wrote Dylan, "I wish I could read German.") Vernon also introduced Dylan to Spanish poetry this summer: "I went over to Bishopston", he wrote to Francis in September, "taking with me Lorca & a book of Welsh translations from Taliesin . . . We read a lot of Lorca which is grand—I found I knew about half of it by heart . . ." He helped Dylan write a short appreciation of T. S. Eliot for the Harvard University magazine, as he had helped him with his contribution to the Auden Double Number of *New Verse*. ("Congratulations on Auden's seventieth birthday", was its characteristic conclusion.)

The poems Dylan had written were *On No Work of Words Now*, *The Tombstone Told When She Died*, *A Saint About to Fall* and the *Birthday Poem* ("Twenty-four years remind the tears of my eyes"). "I cannot describe my excitement when I saw [it] for the first time on a postcard", Vernon wrote in his edition of the *Letters*. Vernon suggested that *A Saint About to Fall* should be called *Poem in the Ninth Month*, and this title was used at the poem's first printing in *Poetry* (London); when it appeared in *The Map of Love*, and later in *Collected Poems*, the first line was used as title.

Dylan was also at this time working on the stories which were later to be collected in *Portrait of the Artist*. These stories represented a real change in both style and attitude, a change observed by the only critic who at that time was following Dylan's work as closely as Dylan himself.

> In the prose, too, (wrote Vernon) there came recurrent moments of severe self-appraisal, moments when what had seemed to be a masterpiece at the time of writing appeared in retrospect to be only a tour-de-force. The highly charged language of the symbolic stories reached its climax in what was to be his most ambitious story, the opening of which he left as a fragment called *In the Direction of the Beginning*. He told me after this that he would never again write a story of that kind, and at the same time his verse underwent a profound change, not exactly of language, but of approach. The change was, I think, heralded by the little poem which begins:
>
> > Once it was the colour of saying . . .
>
> This, and the other poems of *The Map of Love*, showed that, while he had now resolved to write only stories about real people, his poetry had also moved in the direction of the living voice.

If it was the end of an era in Dylan's work, it was also the end of an era in his life. ("You know I'm going to be a father in January", he wrote to Vernon.) And the war was coming nearer. But however dramatic the new life, however brilliant the new work, the old life and the old work had been good. It was the Laugharne days that Vernon commemorated in his poem *To a Shell:*

> At last, beautiful shell,
> Lie there crushed: but the sea
> Cannot obliterate yet
> Faith I remember well:
> A house facing the sea.

Hard and bitterly
Though waves beat on that wall
From the swirling quicksands of debt,
I swear that it cannot fall.

Nor can you drag those words,
Confident in their day,
Down to the unknown deep.
I have a net whose cords
Gather the fallen day
And make the forgotten stay
In all but the detail death
Moves to the realm of sleep,
So strong is the pledge of breath.

And though the magical dice,
Loaded for nothing, toss
All to perdition, left
In darkness, held in a vice,
No white breaker can toss
All to a total loss.
Still the relic will hold,
Caught in a secret cleft,
Tenderer light than gold.

All I remember, all
Of the locked, unfolding days
Where tomorrow's treasure shines.
Fragile nautilus caul,
Tell the fingers of days:
'Find me. Enter the praise
Of Eden's morning, inlaid
With dazzling, intimate lines.
Touch, and the world will fade.'

CHAPTER SIX: THE EDGE OF THE ABYSS

He told me that he was writing a new poem . . . It was to be called 'DEATHS AND ENTRANCES' because, he said, it was all he had ever written about or wanted to write about. — V.W.

1939 began with death and birth. On the twenty-eighth of January Yeats died; on the thirtieth Dylan's son was born.

Vernon was devastated by the news of Yeats' death. He wrote at once to Francis:

"I expect you were awake last night too. What is to be said? Yeats himself has said the last word:

'Now that my ladder's gone,
I must lie down where all the ladders start
In the foul rag-and-bone shop of the heart.'

. . . Yesterday, before hearing the news, I had talked to my father a lot about Yeats's illness, about his going to Menton for the winter. I had no actual premonition of immediate death, yet the news of his death came as no surprise. I was in this room . . . and mother shouted through the partition. I said 'I know' quite evenly. When you rang up I was still in a pretty incoherent state."

But the incoherence became coherent: emotion was subjected to the discipline of words:

I lean down, crying: 'Touch me, lay hold on my Spring,
Reach up, for I have loosened, tearing your skies,
Fountains of light, ages of listening!'
But the bound hands are folded, the fold its word denies.

What shudder of music unfulfilled vibrates?
What draws to a dust-grain's fall most distant stars?
In the last taper's light what shadow meditates?
What single, athletic shape never cast on wall or vase?

What shudder of birth or death? What shakes me most?
Job his Maker answering, the Stricken exclaiming 'Rejoice!'
Gripping late in the shifting moment giant Earth, making
Earth a ghost,
Who heard a great friend's death without a change of voice.

Dylan and Caitlin were at Blashford, in Hampshire, waiting for the birth of their child. Dylan wrote to Vernon when the baby was two days old, ''I'm sorry Yeats is dead. What a loss of the great poems he would write. Aged 73, he died in his prime.'' He too looked back over the year that was gone, in a small poem sent to Vernon in February with the provisional title of *January 1939*. This was the famous poem beginning:

> Because the pleasure-bird whistles after the hot wires,
> Shall the blind horse sing sweeter?

over which James Agate was so gleeful in his column in the *Daily Express.* The image of the singing horse came from a dream of Dylan's, in which a horse stood in a cage made of wires which gradually became red-hot, on which a man standing by said, ''He sings better now''. But I wonder if the poem was not also unconsciously influenced by Hardy's *The Blinded Bird*:

> So zestfully canst thou sing?
> And all this indignity,
> With God's consent, on thee!
> Blinded ere yet a-wing
> By the red-hot needle thou,
> I stand and wonder how
> So zestfully thou canst sing!

Dylan's poem shows the poet ''an enamoured man alone with the twigs of his eyes'' turning ''to stare at an old year''. And although he says ''this present grace'' over ''the past table'', the future seems to be at best enigmatic and, at worst, sinister. Indeed Dylan wrote to Bert Trick in March 1939, ''We're all moving away. And every single decisive action happens in a blaze of disappointment.'' If Dylan, twenty-four years old, not two years married, and the father of a six-week-old son really felt this, the years that were gone must have meant more to him than those to come. Constantine FitzGibbon comments:

Dylan's nostalgia for the past, for that lost paradise of innocence which we all carry with us throughout lives that are
seldom innocent and never paradisiac, became henceforth an

ever stronger theme in his writing . . . And in his later poems, which he once defined to a journalist as 'statements on the way to the grave', this emotion is of far greater complexity, and nostalgia itself becomes an inadequate word with which to define it.

Still, for the time being, he was coming back to Laugharne, and Vernon waited impatiently for his return.

> Dylan will be in Bishopston at Easter for a day (he wrote to Francis in March,) with Caitlin and his boy . . . He's bringing out a book of poems and 7 stories with a portrait by John, to cost 7/6. 'A Prospect of the Sea' was refused on the grounds of its 'unwarrantable moments of sensuality'. Can you beat that? It's like telling somebody to write with his hands in a muff . . . it convinces me that publishers' heads are full of sawdust, that their eyes are really buttons.

Vernon had no time for editors, publishers, critics or just plain readers who did not appreciate Dylan's work. Long after Dylan's death he wrote about the two "birth poems" at the end of *The Map of Love*:

> The second of these two poems was to be a dialogue between an unborn child and its mother, and it was about this that Robert Graves, who has so many children but doesn't seem to know how they are born, showed such ignorance and obtuseness in his Clark lecture.

Dylan's work was sacrosanct; but even his actions were not to be lightly criticised. Because he had not heard a broadcast of Dylan's, Francis was called "You wart, blain, pimple, boil, pig's trotter, skunk's tail, swollen toe, female flea . . ." but when Dylan failed to turn up in Swansea for the performance of Vernon's masque *The Influences*, Vernon made many, often incompatible, excuses.

Two performances were given by the Swansea Little Theatre, on the 6th and 7th of July. On the 4th Dylan wrote:

> This is to tell you, with great regret, that we *may* not be able to come to your play. If Hughes can come . . . then we'll be able to; if not, not. I thought I'd some money this week, but

bills took it at once & now we couldn't afford to go to Carmarthen even.

Vernon wrote to Francis on the 6th, before the first performance, "I've just had a wire from Dylan to say he's coming." But in the event, although Richard and Frances Hughes turned up, Dylan did not. A letter to Frances on the 7th says, "Last night was momentous. The Masque was glorious . . . How I wish you could have been there! Nearly everyone was, except Dylan and Caitlin who were kept away by horrible colds . . .". To make matters worse, Dylan did visit Bishopston for two weeks almost immediately after the Masque, while Vernon was in Scotland on his annual vacation. Yet in a broadcast interview with Robin Holmes in 1957, when Holmes commented, "In your book [of Letters] he does treat you rather carelessly on occasion, apparently—he didn't for instance come to the Masque?", Vernon was quick to defend Dylan by saying, "Well, that was a question of money with the Masque; unfortunately he ran out of funds, he would certainly have come . . .".

But in the spring of 1939 all that was in the future: Dylan was back in Wales.

> I'm incredibly happy, too . . . (Vernon wrote to Francis on April 15th,) Yes, and you must congratulate me as well, because I'm now a father. Don't be alarmed. Dylan made me godfather to his child, and he was proxy for me. He rushed into the house last Saturday & asked me to come to the christening but I had to perform my blessing by proxy. I got the christening present for Llewelyn yesterday—a silver spoon and fork,—very lovely. I'll go to Laugharne next weekend, I expect.

While Dylan had been in Ringwood, Vernon had not been unmindful of him, and had sent a Compendium of games for Christmas: but early in January he bought the young couple another present. He told Francis that he had telephoned Dylan ("those soft Cambridge accents sliding from Wales", said Dylan) ". . . about a wireless which I suddenly bought for him at a sale last week. He's always wanted one & I saw it & rushed in & got it. It's an A-C-D-C."

God knows what Vernon, the most unmechanical of
men, thought those initials stood for. "Whether it will
work at Laugharne or not I don't know . . ."

Dylan didn't know either, nor did the "expert" who
came round to Sea View to instal it.

> Is the wireless set, please, A.C. or D.C.? (wrote Dylan path-
> etically). The expert here can't tell and daren't test it until
> he knows for certain; he might blow it up. (It was still not in-
> stalled by the middle of May). We still haven't had the wire-
> less set up in our house yet. It's still in Billy Williams's
> —he's the local electrician. He wanted me to get hold of the
> set's book of instructions for him, or, at any rate, a little 3
> plug lead which is supposed to go in at the back of the
> machine but which wasn't among the parts you gave me. . .

But the difficulty with the wireless was of no importance: what was important was that Dylan and poetry were
together again in Vernon's life. "I spent last weekend with
Dylan at Laugharne", he wrote to Francis on the 21st of
May, "He's much bigger all round—12 stone 8—but otherwise very much the same. We had a long confab. with
Richard Hughes in which I took no part. And I cycled home
in the dark without a lamp of any kind."

The baby Llewelyn was a new element in the visits.
Although Vernon was over thirty, he had no young married
friends or relatives, and therefore no acquaintance with
babies or small children. Bachelors are usually either cyn-
ical or romantic about marriage: Vernon was romantic.
Caitlin had been aureoled with Dylan's glory; now their
son shone in its rays. Caitlin suckling her baby became
almost a Madonna in Vernon's eyes, and indeed he named
a sonnet written at this time *The Mother and Child*:

> Let hands be about him white, O his mother's first,
> Who caught him, fallen from light through nine months' haste
> Of darkness, hid in the worshipping womb, the chaste
> Thought of the creature with its certain thirst.
> Looking up to her eyes declined that made her fair
> He kicks and strikes for joy, reaching for those dumb springs.
> He climbs her, sinks and his mouth under darkness clings
> To the night-surrounded milk in the fire of her hair.

She drops her arm, and, feeling the fruit of his lips,
Tends him cunningly. O what secrets are set
In the tomb of each breath, where a world of light in eclipse
Of a darkly worshipping world exults in the joy she gave
Knowing that miracle, miracle to beget,
Springs like a star to her milk, is not for the grave.

It is a far cry from Dylan's own "anguish and carrion",
"the infant forever unfree"; to Vernon it is the child that is
miraculous, to Dylan in spite of "the time-bomb town",
"the skull of the earth . . . barbed with a war of burning
brains and hair", it is the world itself that is, or could have
been, a miracle: "the endless beginning of prodigies
suffers open". But both poems are "full of exultation and
mystery . . ." they contain metaphysical, not social comment.

Vernon's attitude to Llewelyn was one of wary rev-
erence; he took his duties as godfather very seriously. He
sent money when he could, always remembered Christmas and birthday presents, and, when he wrote poems for
or about Dylan and Llewelyn, the payments were faithfully remitted to Laugharne. The first poem for his god-
child was to accompany the spoon which had been his
christening present:

There in the velvet lies
Near your blue eyes,
Enclosed in its own silences
A spoon . . .

It mirrors back a wave,
Silver and grave,
From expectation's haunted cave,
In which your bigger eyes one day may see
A tall house leaning, open to the sea.

And there the sudden tide
Flooding the wide
Mud-hollows at the Castle's side,
Pounds tongues with light, and, breaking language down,
Brings to our ears the Portreeve's fishing-town.

Of eight short Poems for Llewelyn, which appeared in
the August 1940 issue of *Life and Letters Today*, the third
describes the "frail boards" sheltering the little family
always in Vernon's heart and mind:

> Fingers of poverty faintly knock.
> Here, where is written in breath
> Blake's immortality sleeping in the rock,
> For a father who trusts in death.

The fourth poem holds a reference to one of Dylan's own
letters, in which he had written, ". . . the ravens,—soft,
white, silly ravens—will feed us":

> Softer than all things but
> The youngest leaves,
> Cheek in love's shade lies safe; your eyes are shut
> Beneath the faint lids nobody believes
> Can hide the sailing heavens
> But he who stands
> By unicorn and tree beneath the ravens
> Whose claws have dropped their bread into his hands.

The sixth poem, six lines long, paints a tiny domestic
scene in Sea View:

> Birds I remember, solitary birds.
> While I was looking, osiers wreathing
> Your cradle hung. That golden wife
> Stooped, and left in the room three words,
> Alone here breathing:
> "A little life".

These poems were written for Llewelyn's first birthday;
for his second, *Llewelyn's Chariot* (although it did not
appear in *Life and Letters Today* until March 1943). This
poem originated in an occasion when Vernon slept in the
same room as Llewelyn, aged about eighteen months. The
baby's cot was on the other side of the room from the vis-
itor's bed; but at dawn Vernon woke to find the cot, driven
on its castors by the baby's strong agitations of its bars,
bumping up against the bed, and Llewelyn staring at him
from enormous blue eyes. He saw the voyage as another

Argosy, and the child's gold hair as the golden fleece. The
poem ends:

> And I, your listener, stopped on the stairway of breath,
> Awake, in the stranger's bed, in the cold, high room,
> Calling the sea from Leviathan hollows of earth,
> I watch them, castaway toys, while you drive and boom
> Your course in the cot to my bed, with the speed of ice,
> The giant mirror, the trumpet ringed with a bell
> Till naked you stand, gold-fleeced, shaping, a shell,
> All seas to your colour, Llewelyn, child above price.

(It was to this poem that Dylan was referring when, five
years later in the Boar's Head at Carmarthen, having been
asked to leave because of the noise and disruption caused
among the diners by his small son, he said ruefully ''Llewelyn, child below mice!'')

When Llewelyn was three years old Vernon wrote the
little poem *A Child's Birthday* (which was later published
in *Horizon*, then in *The Lady with the Unicorn*.) A birthday poem which, as far as I know, was never published,
was a pleasant acrostic, in which the initial letters of all
the words read LLEWELYN THOMAS, whether one reads
from the beginning or the end.

To My Godson

> Life's leaven: eleven. Wake early, Llewelyn.
> You nearly touch Heaven. O morning and song!
> Silence and music of happiness telling
> Name you love's Easter: Wake early. Live long.

And when Vernon visited Dylan on the first of September, 1939 he saw the war itself in relation to the child,
and wrote the sonnet *Infant Noah*, which begins:

> Calm the boy sleeps, though death is in the clouds.

In spite of the darkening shadow of war, the summer of
1939 was a happy one for Vernon. He went to Laugharne as
often as he could, not only to read and talk about poetry,
for that went on as naturally as breathing when the two
were together, but to walk on the sands, to drink in the
pub, to sit in the sunny living-room in the evening while

Llewelyn was being fed, bathed and put to bed: to listen to
Dylan reading many of the stories for *Portrait of the Artist*:

> The stories released a stream of humorous invention which
> Dylan had kept out of his poetry but which was very much a
> part of himself . . . My only objection to the *Portrait of the
> Artist* stories was the title. I thought the book ought to be
> called *One Warm Saturday* after the last story. But Dylan was
> firm. Besides, his publishers had said that it was a good sell-
> ing title. I could not see how the stories, as reproductions of
> his boyhood, could be improved; but he used to say that
> although he was very glad he had written them they could not
> compare with Joyce's *Dubliners*. Perhaps not. But I do not
> believe for a moment that Joyce could have written *The
> Peaches*, *The Fight*, or *Extraordinary Little Cough*.

Sometimes Vernon would read to Dylan; Yeats, Kierkegaard (who, he said "pierced Dylan deeply"; but I have
my doubts), Rilke—they spent a whole sunny afternoon in
an ivy-covered recess in Laugharne Castle reading the
Duino Elegies. Dylan admired Rilke as a poet, but called
him "a very odd boy indeed". Occasionally Vernon would
read Dylan extracts from the famous Italian grammar.
This book had been found on the second-hand shelves in
the Charing Cross Road some years before, and immediately took an honoured place among the Watkins
family heirlooms. Its title-page declared it to be a Manual
of Conversation English-Italian, with the Italian figured
pronunciation for English Tourist in Italy, by Prof.
CARLO BARONE. Unlike most compilers of manuals,
who prefer to guard their anonymity, *il professore* Barone
scattered traces of his personality with a lavish hand
throughout his book—and such a personality! Unspeak-
ably satisfied with his grasp of English conversation, he
was complacently aware that his errors (if errors there
could be) made the language he loved second only to his
own Italian more rich, more colloquial, more flexible than
any of its users before. And Vernon and Dylan, who also
loved the English language, read and re-read his great book,
and learned much from it. It is impossible to end this chap-

ter without quoting a little from Professor Barone's masterpiece.

It opens with an announcement that the Italian *abbici* has twenty-two letters, five wowels and seventeen consoonants. To show that this is no mere misprint, but a willed improvement on the language, the chapter on WOWELS then begins: and the word is so spelt (consistency is Barone's strong point) throughout the book (as in "if the werb ends in a wowel, the initial letter of the pronoun is doubled and the last wowel of the werb lose the accent.") Even in mere grammatical examples his personal style revealed itself: Dylan was particularly fond of the negative imperatives, the first somewhat rarified, "let them not chock with thirst"; the next, as he pointed out, simple, direct, and full of personal anguish, "Do not let him sing!" He felt too that as an example of the pluperfect, "He had had a hat" could hardly be bettered.

The chapter entitled Nomenclature fascinated him especially the section on Parts of the Human Body, the end of which, he said, the critics might easily take as notes for one of his own early poems: it went thus:

> The bones, the marrow, the nerves, an articulation;
> Humours, the blood, the bile, spittle;
> Tears, sweat, milk, urine,
> The corpse.
> A skeleton.

He threatened, before his child's birth, to name it only from Barone's section on Proper Names, where he could choose from such names (in delicious juxtaposition) as: Bab, Balthasar, Hilairy, Hippolyt, Hug [sic] and Hyacinthus; Theobald, Tommy, Urban and Ulric. (Vernon's sister suggested that, if the baby proved to be twins, they should be named Ferocity and Insanity.)

Having studied the vocabularies, the earnest tourist was invited to commit to memory certain "preparatory phrases", designed to bring together what he had learned about grammar and words. Of these Dylan's favourite was the memorable sequence:

Let me love my duty
Let her love her grandsons
Let us love our step-daughters
Love you ancestors
Let them love their family
It is your duty to love your parents.
That loving child has ben [sic] sick!

But it is in the little conversational scenes on various occasions and in various localities that Barone's true genius emerges. Not for him dull requests and duller replies: his characters are all aspiring Oscar Wildes, his ripostes sparkle. Even the paper-seller ("Sir, we have of the Times, the Telegraph, and the Tit-bits") has a certain flourish. The tramway conductor is formidable:

Here is your ticket: take care about not lose it; if a controller should arrive he would let pay to you a double ticket.
Conductor, will you let stop or no? I have sounded twice and the mechanician does not stop!
And it is just. We have many stations for stopping for which one is not here.

The telephone operator too burns with a hard gem-like flame:

Miss, give me, please a communication.
There's!
Are you there?
Why, which number do you vish?
Give me please the 21065.

— — — —

Miss! They have taken away the communication.
Certainly. Are already passed the five minutes.

Dylan and Vernon both agreed that Barone's masterpiece was the scene at the dentist's—a view shared, incidentally, by John Lennon in the sixties. He used the scene, transcribed verbatim (except for a few additions of his own which greatly detracted from its impact) in his book *In His Own Write*. Dylan liked to take the part of the dentist, always with a different voice. Vernon made a sheepish and giggling patient. (Acting was not his strong point. When he was nineteen he was pressed into being one of the shepherds in a nativity play. His single line was, pointing to the star, "You can see it through the window". He lay awake the night before the performance trying to decide whether to say "*You* can see it through the window", "You *can* see it through the window", "You can *see* it through the window", and so on through all the possible permutations. On the opening night, heavy-eyed and nearly inaudible, he delivered his line flat syllable by syllable in equal measures.)

I have a hollow tooth that makes me suffer dreadfully.
Sit down in that armchair madam, throw your head back and open your mouth wide. Ho!
Your mouth is pretty clear of teeth!
Alas! I have but eight left.
Then you have lost twen-tyfour.
Impossible!

— — — — —

Let me see the tooth. Is it that one.
Yes sir! Could you not stop it up.
Stopping up teeth is only a palliative.
You will pull it out for me then?
No madam. I will extract it.
But that is very painful!
Not at all. It is a very easy operation, even not unaccompanied with a certain pleasure . . . when it is over. Come, be courageous.
But! sir . . .
Let me only take out the cotton you have put in the hollow of the tooth.—Crack! there it is.
But sir, I was anxious to keep that tooth.
That was impossible. It is black and decayed. Besides you have none but old stumps in your mouth.

When Dylan went to what he called "a very posh dentist" just before going to America for the first time, he sent Vernon some grinning miniature photographs with comments on the back and, in one case, across the face on the print. One read "I have none but old stumps in my mouth!"

The finale of the Barone performance was always Going
to Bed:

> I confess that I am very tired. I am going to undress and get to
> bed directly: in five minutes I shall be no more of this world.
> Have you closed the shutters?
> Yes sir, but perhaps you had better leave them open.
> Why so?
> To see the sun the sooner when you wak [sic].
> I declare myself unworthy to see the orb of day!
> All I know now is that I am ready to fall with sleep.
> Draw the curtains of my bed . . .
> O blissful bed! Blessed be the man who invented beds.
> That is your evening prayer?
> My dear friend, you bore me considerably.
> Let me sleep.

"My dear friend, you bore me considerably", was often
used by Dylan to defuse an argument over poetry when it
became too heated. He could reject criticism of his own
poems very tolerantly: it was Vernon who might flare up if
Dylan suggested emendations.

Another favourite occupation was to revise or improve
lines from well-known poems. "Nobbly, nobbly, Cape St.
Vincent," was one, "My name is Oswald J. Mandias, King
of Kings," another. "It was a summer evening,/Old
Kafka's work was done," was a third. And there were
always the original works of which each poet had to compose an alternate line. One of these was an interminable
ballad called *The Cosmopolitan Secret Agent*, which had a
new verse added every time anyone could think of a different country, shire or town. One verse will suffice to
show its soporific quality:

> I'd like to lurk in the woods with a Turk,
> I'd like to sit on a Lapp.
> I'd like to lie with an Austrian spy,
> I'd like to Nippon a Jap.

Occasionally they would compose slightly pornographic
quatrains, which Dylan one day suggested they should
send to the editor of the children's comic *Puck*: "we could

say we'd misread the title.'' Or they would make plans for the joint editorship of a periodical to be called *Stand*, which should accept only obscene poems and articles.

These were happy times, in spite of the fact that Europe was on the edge of the abyss: neither Dylan nor Vernon would ever be so carefree again.

CHAPTER SEVEN: CHANGES

Wait for no second Spring in Bishopston Valley.
Once, once only it breaks.—V.W.

Two weeks before war was declared *The Map of Love* was published. Dylan sent Vernon an advance copy. ''My book couldn't have come out in a viler month'', he wrote ''. . . This war, trembling over on the edge of Laugharne, fills me with such horror & terror & lassitude . . .'' Not only had he achieved a precarious happiness, as he told his father ''out of nothing'', but the child in him was terrified and the poet deeply sensitive at the prospect of appalling suffering, his own or that of any human being.

On the 3rd September Thomas Taig, of the English Department at the University College of Swansea, and the producer of *The Influences*, drove Vernon down to Laugharne.

There were a lot of soldiers in the pub there, and some deserters were drinking with the escorts who had come to collect them and who had practically decided to desert, too. The room in the pub on that evening was one of the most confused rooms I have ever seen. Outside it was the hill, Laugharne Castle, and the landscape that Dylan would write about in 'Over Sir John's Hill' and the last poems. He loved it, and he hated everything to do with the war; and he knew that very soon he would have to decide whether to register as a conscientious objector or for military service. Dylan did, in fact, make this decision in a rather unexpected way. He felt that it would be best and most logical to be a conscientious objector, but he had to attend a tribunal for objectors in Wales as a witness. As each objector came forward, he was asked on what grounds he objected to military service, and in each case a mean little voice answered ''ligious'. Each was then asked what he was prepared to do, and each answered, in an even meaner little voice, 'Nothing'. When Dylan left this court he felt that one door was closed to him, and later, when his own turn came, he confessed to me that he had signed for the army, but as a never-fighter. 'Talk about the lads of the land',

81

he said, describing his call-up. 'Most of them were twisted with rheumatism, and none looked under fifty. The man next to me said he would join the Navy as he wanted to fly. He was classified D4, and I was C3'.

In the event, Dylan was exempted from military service, but not until the early summer of 1940: at the beginning of the war he suffered the same anxieties as all his friends. The Bank would not release Vernon, and, although he registered, he was put on deferred service. This was the period of the 'phony war', and so, for a little while longer, life went on much as usual.

Keidrych Rhys, the editor of *Wales*, was married in Llanstephan at the beginning of October, and Dylan was to be his best man. "Have you got a respectable suit you can lend me, or, rather, trust me with?" he wrote to Vernon. "I'll return it, unegged, straight after the wedding—the next day, really, I can't undress in the church porch." Vernon sent him, as a gift, not a loan, his last year's bank suit. "It's grand of you to let me keep it:" wrote Dylan, "I am now ready for all sartorial occasions, so long as at some of them I can appear in jersey & corduroys & at others in a smart brown suit, slightly open in the middle, with its pockets full of rice." Incidentally, this must have been the only time when Dylan actually succeeded in fulfilling his role as best man: at Constantine FitzGibbon's wedding he turned up only for the reception, and at Vernon's he did not turn up at all. Vernon once suggested that a small society might be formed whose members would be people for whom Dylan had failed to be best man.

Nor did the war stop the reading and writing of poetry. In June Vernon had stayed in Laugharne and had recited to Dylan "when we were walking down a hill" the great Yeats poems which appeared posthumously in the *London Mercury: Lapis Lazuli, The Statues, Long-Legged Fly*, and *News for the Delphic Oracle*. In November Dylan asked Vernon to send him copies of them for a proposed reading to the English Club at Cambridge, together with some poems of his own. Vernon had also introduced Dylan to

the poems of John Crowe Ransom; they both preferred
Captain Carpenter and *Judith of Bethulia* to any others.

Vernon was also working on his poem *The Windows*
(later printed in *The Ballad of the Mari Lwyd* as *The Windows of Breath*.) Dylan did not care for it: he called it "a
serious failure—I mean it is a serious poem which fails"
and (using its own words) "a camphored elegy". Vernon
took criticism far more angrily than Dylan did, but he
largely rewrote the poem. Dylan himself was working on
Once Below a Time. This was almost the only one of his
poems which Vernon did not care for: he thought it cocky
and flippant without being witty, and he really disliked
the tarted-up cliché, even when it occurred in a poem as
beautiful as *Fern Hill* in the form of "happy as the heart
was long." What he did like was the Nansen line in the
poem:

> Cold Nansen's beak on a boat full of gongs.

Nansen was an old hero of his, and the subject of a prize-
winning poem written at Repton.

The Christmas of 1939 Dylan, Caitlin and Llewelyn
spent at Bishopston. Dylan wrote on December 13th,
"What do I want for Christmas? Oh, that's nice. I want a
war-escaper—a sort of ladder, I think, attached to a
balloon—or a portable ivory tower or a new plush womb to
escape back into. Or a lotion for invisibility." He might be
funny about the war, but he was in fact appalled by what he
called "world lunacy". He could be serious about its horror only perhaps in verse; and that Christmas he told Vernon that he felt he must continue to celebrate in his poetry

> the praise of everything that war crushed and rejected. He set
> himself to re-state the holiness of life in the scenery of Hell
> and irrational death . . . the changes he made were, as in all
> the late poetry, away from ironical statement and in the
> direction of religious truth.

When the family left Bishopston to stay with Caitlin's
mother in Ringwood Dylan was working on *There Was a
Saviour*. This, a poem about invasion, was the first of the

magnificent war poems which afterwards included *A Refusal to Mourn, Holy Spring, Ceremony After a Fire Raid* and *Among Those Killed in the Dawn Raid was a Man Aged a Hundred.* There is no doubt that the later ones are greater than the first; are, indeed, among the great war poems of the English language; but of *There Was a Saviour* Vernon wrote:

> This was really the first of the entirely assonantal poems. Dylan had from the first preferred the method of mixing rhymes and half-rhymes, but his test for a rhyme was that you should not expect it. He certainly did not like writing in unrhymed form. He welcomed obstacles and difficulties. But he also did not like, as he once told me, finding his rhymes labelled for him like the stations on railway-tickets. He wanted to preserve a strictness of choice in language with which direct rhyme sometimes interfered. So he resorted to assonance and dissonance and built his stanzas on a fabric of exact language in which the line-endings were musically and mathematically balanced, and enhanced, rather than re-produced, the sound that had gone before.

There Was a Saviour is, possibly, a poem for poets—at least for those who thought poetry enough, whose temptation might have been to see human suffering as another subject for art:

> O you who could not cry
> On to the ground when a man died
> Put a tear for joy in the unearthly flood
> And laid your cheek against a cloud-formed shell:
> Now in the dark there is only yourself and myself.

It was peculiarly a poem for Vernon and for Dylan himself.

In answer to Vernon's appreciation, Dylan wrote in March 1940, ''I'm so glad you liked [it], that you thought it was one of my best . . . about line 3 of the last verse, you're right as can be, and somehow I must make 'death' the second word . . . Your criticism's always terribly suggestive, & in that particular 'death line' you showed quite clearly to me the one big misbalance in the poem. Ta.'' The 'death line' was originally

Deaths of the only ones, our never found.

It was reworked as

Brave deaths of only ones but never found.

In the days when figures in banks went through the hands and heads of the clerks, and not through machines, the twice-yearly stock-taking meant that the clerks had to work until the figures were complete. On December 31st, 1939, Vernon came home exhausted from the bank just in time to hear a midnight broadcast from his father's old home, Tynewydd at Taff's Well. The Mari Lwyd—The Grey Mare—was a horse's skull, or sometimes a horse's head modelled in wood, decorated with ribbons and carried from house to house. The carriers, singers and impromptu versifiers, challenged the inmates to a rhyming contest. They could be kept out of a house as long as a rhyme could be found: if the inmates failed to reply, however, the Mari Lwyd and her supporters could claim right of entry, food and drink.

A condition of extreme exhaustion may sometimes have almost hallucinatory effects. Vernon, supine in an armchair in the firelit room, had a strange vision of a horse's skull "followed and surrounded by all kinds of drunken claims and holy deceptions". The next day he began to write his *Ballad of the Mari Lwyd.*

There are many possible interpretations of the Ballad, in which the inmates of the house are called the Living and those outside the Dead. But it is certain that it is in some way an attempt by Vernon to come to terms with the dichotomy of Dylan's nature, his "drunken claims and holy deceptions". It was not a dichotomy he could bring himself to recognise in life; his friend was always "good", only occasionally wearing the "masks" of selfishness, indifference, dishonesty, unreliability—and always wearing them unwillingly, because they were demanded by the insatiable public. But art concerns itself only with truth: Dylan had become of inconceivable importance to Vernon's life and poetry, and he must be examined by the rigorous standards of art.

In the Ballad, and in its sequel the *Ballad of the Outer Dark*, no conclusion is reached: at first the Living repel the Dead, and finally the Dead break in and turn the Living out into the dark, but they are never brought together. The only suggestion of a reconciliation is a plea that there should be forgiveness between them. Perhaps it is all that can be said for the apparently irreconcilable.

The first draft of the Ballad was finished in March 1940, and although Vernon wrote of it with great excitement to Dylan, he did not send it to him, but waited until Dylan and Caitlin were again in Bishopston in May. They were there temporarily because of a crisis in their financial affairs. "I've had to sneak my family away from our home in Carmarthenshire", he wrote to Stephen Spender, "because we could no longer obtain any credit and it was too awful to try to live there, among dunning and suspicion, from hand to mouth when I knew the hand would nearly always be empty."

Dreary though it must have been for Dylan and Caitlin to live with, and on, his parents, it was a month of unmitigated bliss for Vernon. There was croquet again, the reading, writing and discussion of poetry, walks along the cliffs and through Bishopston Valley and once an expedition to Rhossili, where Wyn Lewis drove them. They walked out to the end of the Worm, a rocky promontory jutting out from Rhossili beach, the scene of *Extraordinary Little Cough*, and were nearly cut off by the tide. Dylan and Vernon were walking some way behind Wyn and Caitlin when they first became aware that the pools between the Worm and the mainland were rapidly filling up. Wyn and Caitlin began to run and managed to jump across; Dylan, podgy and soon beginning to pant, became almost frantic at the prospect, not of spending eight hours on the Worm, but of spending eight hours on the Worm while Caitlin and the handsome Wyn were on the mainland. Kneedeep in waves and completely breathless, he was finally dragged by Vernon on to the dry rocks. When they had climbed back up to the Downs, each of the four took a

Dylan, Wyn Lewis and Vernon at Rhossili.
'. . . you nearly caught us napping on the Worm . . .' June 1940.

photograph of the other three: Dylan still serious, almost sullen, at the narrowness of his escape from jealousy.

It was during this period too that Vernon, Dylan and Caitlin went to a performance of *The Marriage of Figaro* in the Empire Theatre. Before the performance Dylan quoted to Vernon the first two lines of a new poem which he was going to call *Deaths and Entrances*:

> On almost the incendiary eve
> Of several near deaths

and said that he was going to call his next book by the same title "because that is all I ever write about or want to write about". Later, in November, he brought the poem to Heatherslade and spent the evening completing it. The final line—"Looms the last Samson of your Zodiac—" was based on a suggestion of Vernon's, and Dylan remained uncertain about it; because, he said, "'zodiac' is a Watkins word, not a Thomas word". The last lines originally held a hyena image suggested by one of his favourite passages from *Nightwood*:

> 'For the lover, it is the night into which his beloved goes', he said, 'that destroys his heart; he wakes her suddenly, only to look the hyena in the face that is her smile, as she leaves that company . . .'

But Dylan was not satisfied with that ending either:

> His exposition of the ending was elaborate and detailed. He did not write it down, but he spoke of all the accumulated forces of the projected words, and the weight they had to carry. I still have a work-sheet on which he jotted down some of the images which finally composed the last stanza, and it brings that particular evening to life more clearly than any photograph could have done.

But the evening, and others like it, came to an end. "What a lot of pities we never could arrange longer and noisier evenings:" wrote Dylan in June when he was briefly back in Laugharne,

> noisy with our own poems, and even with poor Yeats's or done Pound's . . . But we had our moments, I heard *Baille's*

Strand [one of Yeats last plays] and two, at least, fine ones of
your own, we heard Figaro and "I am" very very high up in
the Empire roof, Beethoven accompanied our croquet, you
nearly caught us napping on the Worm—and what would a
stranger, hearing suddenly, make of that?

There was one more visit to Bishopston before Dylan's
parents left it for ever; but between this one and
that one the "blood-dimmed tide" had rolled in. France
had fallen in June, the Battle of Britain was fought in
August, in the autumn the blitzes began. By September
invasion seemed likely. Dylan, though terrified, was not a
coward. Dr. Daniel Jones says of him, "He dreaded and
avoided pain, but actually sought . . . a confrontation with
injury or danger". He never avoided London during the
bombing raids, nor even during the later V1 attacks. But
for the time being he was safe in John Davenport's house in
Marshfield, near Chippenham, spending the summer with
other artists and musicians. "Davenport & I are writing a
fantastic thriller together, so I haven't done a poem for a
long time although there are 2 I want to write badly: both
nightmares, I'm afraid. Oh Europe etcetera please do be
bettera."

Francis Labeyrie, who had been married in London in
1939, had of course returned to France on the outbreak of
war. At first communications were normal and Vernon
was able to send him each issue of *Life and Letters Today*
as it came out, with letters that always contained news of
Dylan. In September 1939 he wrote from Bayonne, in the
Basses-Pyrenées, "I was glad to read 'The Ballad of the
Rough Sea' and also Dylan's story Extraordinary Little
Cough which seems to me very different from what I read
of him before. I liked it 'a lot'. You will be good to send me
the next copy . . . Life and Letters is a friendly thing when it
comes, and one of the rare things now that keep you from
losing heart." And after receiving the December issue:
"Dylan's story stirs up lots of good memories of him in my
mind, extravagant walks we had together in Swansea,
visits to people living near the Docks, his talk and lots of
eccentric things so good to remember: personally that's

what I like best in his autobiographical stories. I liked the previous one better than 'The Fight', though. Remember me to him and Caitlin.''

By January 1940 Francis was in the army; remembering Dylan's horror of weapons, he wrote, ''As I am the tallest in our section, I have been entrusted with the ''fusil-mitrailleur'' (light M.G.); tell Dylan it fires 600 shots a minute!'' and later ''Give my love to Poet-Commander Thomas.'' Vernon managed to get a copy of *Portrait of the Artist as a Young Dog* to him before the fall of France. ''It's also Dylan's fault if I did not write to you over the week-end'', Francis wrote, ''I went to Paris and spent my time in the train reading 'One Warm Saturday', 'The Peaches' and 'Where Tawe Flows'. It is a very entertaining book with humour the hell of a damn sight better than Dickens's. It's more easy to apprehend to one remembering Dylan's wise-cracks in actual life and speech. I am glad to recognise in it bits of scenery I know, the Grammar School, the Single-ton, and the Welsh too.''

But the ''bits of scenery'' Francis knew, among them the Grammar School, were soon only a memory. ''I can't imagine Gower bombed'', wrote Dylan from Marshfield. ''High explosives at Pennard. Flaming onions over Pwll-du. And Union Street ashen. This is all too near.''

Vernon had hoped to fly to Paris to the christening of Francis' daughter Danielle, but the Germans were march-ing on Paris and attacking it from the air. Later he was to write *The Broken Sea*, a poem in which sorrow for his god-daughter, ''born in a wailing time'', mingles with sorrow for his own past and the loss of his friend:

> I was going to fly to your christening to give you a cup.
> Here, like Andersen's tailor, I weave the invisible thread.
> The burnt-out clock of St. Mary's has come to a stop,
> And the hand still points to the figure that beckons the house-
> stoned dead.
>
> Child shades of my ignorant darkness, I mourn that moment
> alive
> Near the glow-lamped Eumenides' house, overlooking the
> ships in flight,

Where Pearl White focussed our childhood, near the foot of
Cwmdonkin Drive,
To a figment of crime stampeding in the posters' wind-blown
blight.

I regret the broken Past, its prompt and punctilious cares,
All the villainies of the fire-and-brimstone-visited town.
I miss the painter of limbo at the top of the fragrant stairs,
The extravagant hero of night, his iconoclastic frown.

But Danielle's father could not read the poem, for
silence had fallen on France.

Dylan and Caitlin spent a long time at Bishopston from
Christmas onwards, more poverty-stricken than ever, and
in disgrace with his parents because he had lost his ration-
book. ". . . We've been cooped up here, in little, boiling
rooms, quite broke," he wrote to John Davenport in January. ". . . Today the pipes burst, and Caitlin, in a man's
hat, has been running all day with a mop from W.C. to
flooded parlour, while I've been sitting down trying to
write a poem about a man who fished with a woman for
bait and caught a horrible collection."

This poem was the *Ballad of the Long-Legged Bait*,
written when Vernon was seeing Dylan as often as three or
four times a week—as often as he could, indeed, knowing
that he would soon be called up.

> . . . I saw this poem grow from its first fifteen lines through all
> the stages of its composition. He wrote the four-lined verses
> in pairs. The poem is full of visual imagery. It was so much a
> visual poem that he made a coloured picture for it which he
> pinned on the wall of his room, a picture of a woman lying at
> the bottom of the sea. She was a new Loreley revealing the
> pitfalls of destruction awaiting those who attempted to put
> off the flesh.

Dylan also borrowed Vernon's typewriter "for short,
irregular periods" he wrote rather aggrievedly to Davenport. He can hardly have been aware what a stringent test
of Vernon's love for him it was that he had been allowed to
borrow it at all. Until about 1934 Vernon wrote all his
poems in manuscript; but once he had begun to use a type-

writer (because of the expense of having his poems typed—twenty pages could cost as much as five shillings!) he was rapidly converted. He felt that the poem could only be looked at impersonally in print. Dylan had a similar feeling. "Don't be too harsh to these poems until they're typed;" he had written in March 1938. "I always think typescript lends some sort of certainty: at least, if the things are bad then, they appear to be bad with conviction; in ordinary mss. they look as though they might be altered at any moment." At this time Vernon often made even first drafts of a new poem straight on to the typewriter; to be without it even for "short irregular periods" must have been a real deprivation for him. As soon as his initial training in the R.A.F. was over and he was posted to a station, he retrieved his typewriter from Pennard, and thereafter it went with him until his demobilisation.

In February the centre and some suburbs of Swansea were destroyed by fire-bombs in three night-raids. Vernon, in the Home Guard, watched the glare of the burning town from the heights of Pennard golf-links. Dylan, meeting a friend in the ruins of the Market, said with tears, "Our Swansea is dead".

It was the beginning of the end of their Swansea past. Because of the raids Dylan's parents prepared to move from Bishopston to safer Carmarthenshire. In May Dylan and Caitlin were back in Laugharne, staying in the Castle with Frances Hughes while Richard Hughes was away at sea. Fred Janes, Dan Jones and Tom Warner were in the Army, John Prichard in the Navy, and Vernon had applied for the Field Security Police but had been turned down because he could not ride a motor-bike. Dylan did not care for the armed forces. "I'm glad you wrote, telling the officials you can only just turn on a bathroom tap. Be a censor: pry and erase. Don't be a cyclist or a parachutist or a mine-tester or the first man on the *very* edge of Dover cliffs."

At about this time Dylan was working on a novel, of which he had read the first two chapters to Vernon while he was still at Bishopston. They had discussed possible titles. *The Skins* was not quite right, *A Trader in Skins* or *A Traveller in Skins* might do. Dylan had finally decided on *Adventures in the Skin Trade.* Now, from Laugharne Castle, he wrote, "My prose-book's going well, but I dislike it. It's the only really dashed-off piece of work I remember doing. I've done 10,000 words already. It's indecent and trivial, sometimes funny, sometimes mawkish, and always badly written, which I do not mind so much." A week later, he wrote, "My novel blathers on. It's a mixture of Oliver Twist, Little Dorrit, Kafka, Beachcomber, and good old 3-adjectives-a-penny belly-churning Thomas, the Rimbaud of Cwmdonkin Drive."

Not long after this Vernon was in Laugharne for a weekend:

> . . . I was there when a London publisher's letter arrived, expressing disappointment in the opening chapters of the novel. It was not, ran the letter, the great, serious autobiographical work to which they had looked forward for so long. The manuscript would be returned, and it was hoped that he would offer them something autobiographical, but different, at a later date. Dylan re-read the letter with amused indignation. He was hard up, and a letter of acceptance would have been far more satisfactory. He protested to me that, whatever the publisher said, he thought the book entertaining, and he would not write any kind of solemn rhetoric.
> At this time he used to write mainly in the afternoon, and after lunch he disappeared, and showed me a new part he had written when he emerged for tea. It covered about a page and was extremely funny.

Dylan talked to Vernon a great deal about the plot of this book:

> It was to show what happened to a person, like himself, who took life as it came. This central character, Samuel Bennet, would attract adventures to him by his own unadventurous stillness and natural acceptance of every situation. He would accept life, like a baby who had been given self-dependence. He would have no money, no possessions, no extra clothes, no civilised bias. And life would come to him . . . There was to be a succession of scenes, each being an allegorical layer of life, and at the end of the story the character would be stripped

of all illusion, naked at last. It would be in one way a journey through the Inferno of London, but it would also be a comedy. There is no doubt that, beneath the absurdity of situation which would provide furniture for the scenes, lay the influence and sense of tragedy of Webster's *Duchess of Malfi* and Marlowe's *Doctor Faustus*. Had the novel been finished, it is unlikely that the comic central character of the first chapters would not have been revealed as also a tragic figure.

The novel never was finished, it has only three chapters. What was the "unseen obstacle to his imagination"? Vernon said, in his *Afterword* to the Signet edition, that "the pressure of the anarchy of war itself and the vision of distorted London had taken the place of his half-fictional vision and compelled his imagination forward . . .". This may be so, but I do not think it likely. Some chapters were written after he had already experienced the reality of bombed cities: and in any case Dylan sent the manuscript to a publisher in January 1944 with apparently every intention of completing it. I believe that the real difficulty was the intrinsically impossible premise on which the plot rested; and that this was the story of the dichotomy in Dylan's own life. If a baby were given self-dependence, he would die, because he has no ability to use it; if he could use it, he wouldn't be a baby. This was essentially an autobiographical work, but its central problem could be solved in art no more than it could be in life. Dylan longed to be Samuel Bennet, with freedom but no responsibility; but, unlike his anti-hero, he could not simply remain where he was. Time and Life carried him forward, the split in his nature always widening. Dr. Daniel Jones says, "I cannot imagine how these two parts of his personality could be integrated and survive as one."

Vernon did what he could by recognising only one half of Dylan's nature, and calling the other half a 'mask'. He continually responded to Dylan's entreaties for money—"If you ever have 5 shillings you hate, I shan't"; "If you do have a tiny bit to spare, whether it clinks or tinkles, let alone rustles, *do* send it, Vernon . . . Anything, bled boy, leper, from a penny to a pound"; "See if you can

squeeze another drop from your borrowed-to-death body";
but it was like pouring water into sand.

In the Spring of 1941 T. S. Eliot had accepted Vernon's
first book of poems for Faber and Faber, although he did
not approve of the title *Ballad of the Mari Lwyd.* "It's
dollars to dimes", he wrote, "that outside Wales everyone
will call it *The Ballad of the Marie Lloyd.* She was a great
woman and deserving such a tribute, but here it would be
misleading." Vernon finally settled on a title which Dylan
did not care for. "Faber's are bringing out Vernon's poems
this year", he wrote to John Davenport. "I'm very glad.
Provisionally titled 'Gratitude of a Leper', though I'm not
quite sure myself." "Any more about your leprous collection?" he asked Vernon in May 1941. "Perhaps the volume should be surgically bound. I do hope it comes out
this summer, just before the gas." In fact it was issued in
October, under its original title, after an unexpected last-
minute note from Eliot saying, "I hope it will not grieve
you to return to your first love."

Ballad of the Mari Lwyd was pretty well received by the
critics. It is difficult now to remember, or imagine, the
enormous cachet derived from being a Faber poet (and
even more difficult to envisage, without actually looking
at old newspapers and magazines, the really colossal
amount of space devoted to reviews). The *T.L.S.* gave it a
"Recommended" headline and two columns, referring to
the originality of the poet's imagination and the potency of
his rhythm and imagery. Sheila Shannon in the *Spectator*
reviewed it with Walter de la Mare's *Bells and Grass*, and
spoke of it as "a remarkable collection of poems" with
"original and splendid melodies". All the Welsh papers
were delighted to find a new Welsh poet, and the *Herald of
Wales* gave him three page-length columns, with an
amount of quotation, much of it correct, but for an
unfortunate misprint "O God, the atom has slit [for split]
in Werfel's brain!" that partially satisfied even Vernon,
whose idea of a good review was one hundred per cent
quotation. But although he sent Dylan one of his author's
copies of the *Ballad*, with, of course, an affectionate

inscription, Dylan did not write to acknowledge it, nor did he ever comment on the reviews. There was every excuse for him; he had at last found a regular job in London with Strand Films, but had not found a permanent place to live. For a short time he and Caitlin lived in Hammersmith Terrace, then Caitlin was in a remote village, Talsarn, in Cardiganshire and Dylan commuted between there and London. Then, too, Vernon's long deferred-service came to an end in December 1941, and he was moving about to various training stations: still, a note sent to Heatherslade would always have been forwarded.

Dylan evidently liked the *Ballad*; Constantine Fitz-Gibbon says, ''I do not remember hearing him read any of his contemporaries except Norman Cameron and, much more, Vernon Watkins. He thought very highly of the 'Ballad of the Mari Lwyd', which I heard him read more than once.'' (This is no mean feat, by the way, if Fitz-Gibbon means that Dylan read the whole poem, since it takes well over half an hour to read.) And he was generous with praise for poetry he liked. Yet he let the publication of Vernon's first book go by without a word. Vernon was, as always, quick to excuse him, but he was both hurt and disappointed.

This was the beginning of a subtle change in their relationship. They had always been accustomed to discuss their own or each other's poetry with equal interest: but from now on, although Dylan continued for a few years to send Vernon his work in progress, when Vernon sent his own, Dylan did not comment on it. So he sent no more; whether the war changed this, as it changed so many other things, or whether Dylan would have lost interest in Vernon's poems in any case, Vernon never asked himself. But there was never anyone else with whom he would discuss a poem while he was working on it. He retreated to the poetic solitude he had known before he met Dylan, but he never ceased to regret that

> That strictest, lie-disrobing act
> Testing the poem read

was part of the past now, and would not come again.

CHAPTER EIGHT: WARTIME

In a time of darkness the pattern of life is restored
By men who make all transience seem an illusion . . . —*V.W.*

It was more than a year before Vernon and Dylan met again. Vernon had elected to join the R.A.F. police, because the only vacancies in the Air Force at that time were for policemen and cooks. Vernon thought he would do more damage to the war effort as a cook, "because", he said, "you have to cook if you are a cook, but you don't have to make arrests if you are a policeman". He carried out this policy as well as he could, taking a volume of Kierkegaard or Blake to the railway station, where he had been sent to arrest drunks coming back from leave on the last train, and reading peacefully in the waiting-room until the last drunk had ambled back into camp.

There were other police duties that he found quite pleasant. One was to check that no WAAF left camp wearing her stockings inside out (it was a popular myth that the stockings looked as though they had a finer texture on the wrong side than on the right.) Vernon was not only too shy to look at the WAAFs' legs, but was utterly incapable of telling the right side of a stocking from the wrong; so he let all WAAFs through the gate regardless of what they were wearing, and became in consequence the most popular guard on gate duty: the WAAFs would hang around the gate in an ever-growing crowd until the guard changed and AC2 Watkins came on duty. It also became known that if you "booked in" late, the same policeman would almost certainly be too much absorbed in a book of poems to notice that you had written 23.59 in the book rather than the correct 01.30. This led to gratifying enquiries as to when he would be on duty, and gratifying groans when his leave came round.

Even patrolling the camp at night was not bad. He was at least alone for four hours, and could compose poems in his head as he walked round the perimeter of the camp. Once the officer of the watch, an infant fresh from his OCTU, came trembling into the guardhouse to say that he could not think of a password for the night. "It's all right, sir," Vernon comforted him; "it can be any word—any word at all." "I know that", the officer said despairingly, sinking his head in his hands, "but I *can't think of one.*" Then, too, when he was on night duty, he could not only eat the four hearty meals provided for the guard, but as many of the four hearty meals provided for the day shift as he could stay awake for. For the first (and only) time in his life he weighed more than twelve stone. He first became aware of this in the shower, when he found that he was soaping a perceptible bosom, and a colleague in a neighbouring stall suggested that he should go to the Stores and indent for a brassière.

But there were some duties that were not pleasant and not to be avoided. One was lowering the flag at sunset: if it jammed half-way down, as it often did if Vernon was pulling on the ropes, it was embarrassing to hear the Flight-Sergeant raving under his breath, while the bugler wearily played Taps for the third time. Another job he very much disliked was leaping on the running-board of a visiting Air-Marshal's car and guiding him wherever he wanted to go. Vernon could never find his own way about the camp, being entirely lacking in a sense of direction; when he tried to make for the Ablutions, a few yards away from his own hut, there was no telling where he would end up—the Stores, the Medical Centre, the NAAFI. And even when he found the Ablutions, he could never find his own hut again afterwards. So all he could do on the running-board was to say smartly to the Air-Marshal's driver, "Turn left. Now drive straight on", until he passed someone he could ask for directions. Then he would leap efficiently back, saying, "The camp has been reorganised recently, sir." But it was an anxious time.

While he was stationed at Uxbridge in early 1942— where he came top of the Police Course, partly because of his very high marks in rifle and revolver shooting, but mainly because, whatever his lack of knowledge, he could write literate English, while his course-mates, almost all far better policemen than he, could manage only a few misspelled words—he arranged to meet Dylan in London. He had a day pass, which meant that he had to be back in camp one minute before midnight.

He went up on the train with two men from his hut. When they heard where he was going, they decided that as they had never seen a famous poet, they would go with him. One was an East-end publican, one a regular policeman from Norfolk. They liked Dylan, and Dylan liked them; so much that when the pubs closed he took them on to one of his clubs, perhaps the Mandrake. When midnight struck, they were, like three Cinderellas, far from home. They had to hitch their way back to Uxbridge, and it was nearly two a.m. when they reached the camp. Two of them were pretty drunk, and the third (the Norfolk policeman) was almost incapable: they had had to hold him up between them since they climbed off the lorry. If they booked in, not only would they all be put on a charge for overstaying their leave, but he would be on a further, and more serious, charge.

Vernon, used to swinging himself on to rock-faces, was sure he could break into camp, and persuaded the East-ender that he could too: the regular policeman was lying blissfully unconscious in the pouring rain. After herculean efforts they managed to drag themselves and their passive companion over the fence, avoiding the guard patrol, and pussyfoot their burden through the WAAF camp, forbidden to airmen, which was their point of entry. They dumped him silently into his own hut as dawn was breaking, leaving themselves about an hour to dry their soaked uniform and fake an entry in the booking-in book. The East-ender was immensely grateful and admiring. "Any time you come to my pub, drinks will be on the house", he declared; "I never had such a thing as a poet in my pub before, but now I don't care how many I have."

In the early summer of 1942, Vernon left the RAF police (with the amiable words, "I don't suppose I'll ever meet a bigger bunch of crooks'') and was posted to Bletchley Park. Dr. Daniel Jones has pointed out in *My Friend Dylan Thomas* that "what went on in Bletchley is no longer an official secret; a book has been published on the subject." A book may have been published on Ultra, Enigma, and all that; I have not yet seen any book about what went on in Bletchley for the thousands of us who never got a whiff of Ultra.

When Vernon first arrived there (and indeed when I arrived six months later) all Service personnel were bill-etted in Bletchley itself or in outlying villages; the Service camps were not built until, as I remember, 1943. The atmosphere was at this time very informal; Army, Navy, Air Force, officers and other ranks, British and American, all milled about, worked, ate, went on the transport coaches, to billets, and went to entertainments, together. I believe, indeed, that Service personnel were allowed to wear civilian clothes at this period if they chose; certainly we all did so on leave passes. When the camps were built, this pleasant atmosphere changed: Service people wore uniform, ate in Officers' or Sergeants' or Other Ranks' messes, and, regretfully, carried on guerrilla warfare with the camp personnel who were not allowed into the Park, nor allowed to know what went on there. I should have thought the former arrangement much more likely to result in the keeping of secrets than the latter.

When, many years after leaving Bletchley, I read Constantine FitzGibbon's account of Dylan's first idea for the plot of *Under Milk Wood*, I felt a sense of familiarity which I couldn't at first place.

> "The village was declared insane, anti-social, dangerous. Barbed wire was strung about it and patrolled by sentries, lest its dotty inhabitants infect the rest of the world with their feckless and futile view of life . . . The village is the only place that is left free in the whole world . . . This is not the concentration camp; the rest of the globe is the camp, is mad, and only this little place is sane and happy."

The Park was certainly well fenced in and patrolled and the outside world—that is, the sturdy citizens of Bletchley—

certainly thought its inhabitants dotty. They were, too, most of them; brilliant scholars, intellectuals and cryptographers, but indisputably dotty. They had lived in their own mad worlds for so long that Bletchley Park seemed quite normal to them. In the intervals of decoding, the scholars wrote their reviews for the *TLS*, the chess-players queued up to play twenty simultaneous games with Alexander, the philosophers walked arguing round the lake where the body of a dead duckling, trapped by the neck in a cavity, swayed and floated, the musicians thumped and twanged, the novelists made, like Ibsen, card-indexes or biographies of their characters. The food was eatable, and Bletchley, in spite of being a railway junction, was not bombed. It was an oasis of sanity—or something else—in the warring world.

It suited Vernon. Here nobody thought it strange to write poetry; other people wrote or reviewed it, and most people read it. There were tennis courts, and a permanent table-tennis tournament, and not far away from his billet at New Bradwell was Cowper's Olney, with the river for bathing or boating. Here, too, came Constantine Fitz-Gibbon, Dylan's friend and future biographer; and in the Japanese section was Captain Daniel Jones, of whom Vernon had heard so much, and whom he now met for the first time.

Apocryphal stories were part of the fabric of daily life at the Park, and there were plenty about Captain Jones. How, on the final day of his Officers' Selection Course, a question was propounded to him by a red-faced Colonel: "Officer-Cadet Jones, you are marching along a country road with a small detachment of men when suddenly from an aeroplane overhead enemy parachutists begin to land in the field to your left. At the same time a bus carrying a load of civilians overturns and bursts into flame on the road before you. What is your course of action?" Officer-Cadet Jones did not hesitate for a second. He sprang to attention, and snapped, "Fix bayonets and charge, sir!" "Splendid, splendid", roared the colonel, redder than ever. "That's the sort of quick thinking that will win us the war."

A story that Dylan particularly relished when Vernon recounted it to him was of the occasion when a formidable lady officer, the Head of a Section in the War Office which was the counterpart of Captain Jones' Section at Bletchley, arrived for an inspection in a rather slack interval. Captain Jones and his Section, five or six of them, were refreshing themselves with a brisk paper-balls-and-rubber-bands battle when she opened the door unannounced and stood majestically surveying the scene as paper-balls struck and rebounded from her steely form. "Captain Jones", she said sternly, after a pregnant pause, "I do the same amount of work as you at the War Office with one assistant." "Indeed", said Captain Jones, politely rising from his crouching position behind an overturned filing-cabinet, "and how do you divide the work?"

Vernon had been admiring Dan by proxy, as it were, ever since he had heard of him from Dylan, and, having met him, found a great deal more to admire, in such a polymath. In spite of his immense knowledge and attainments, he was not conceited. ("Was that piece in a minor key?" asked Vernon. "No, the major", said Dan kindly. "*Nearly* right.") He was as much interested as Vernon in poetry, and far more knowledgeable about prose. He knew as many comic stories as Dylan, and many more foreign languages than Vernon, who was fascinated by his explanations of Chinese ideographs, and especially of the incredibly detailed verbs, of which his favourite was "to shell peas secretly at midnight." (Once, when Dan had been visiting him at Stony Stratford and was catching the homeward bus, Vernon shouted in farewell, "Come and have another midnight pea with us sometime!" The crowd of local inhabitants waiting for the next bus were only too evidently not familiar with Chinese verbs. But Vernon was rather good at causing misunderstandings of this kind. One crowded Saturday afternoon, after trying in vain for a long time to attract the attention of the assistant in order to buy a copy of *Lettres Françaises*, he finally bawled over the heads of the suddenly silenced multitude, "Miss! Miss! I say! Do you have French Letters here?")

Vernon and Dan invented a game (or sport, or com-
petition) of which the object was to compose a two-sen-
tence scene or playlet, in which the two lines should
sound identical but have different meanings. But this was
not all: in order to explain the two sentences, some sort of
introduction was necessary. The longer and more complex
the build-up and the shorter the two sentences, the more
triumphant the perpetrator. It grew out of a playlet in
which the opening scene showed King Canute majestically addressing the ocean with the words "Obey, O bay!"
on which his daughter, seeing the royal feet washed by the
disobedient waves, sensibly cautioned him, "No, pa king.
No parking."

Later it rose to such heights as:

Scene: a concert hall. On the platform a symphony
orchestra is tuning up. In the audience a foreign music critic is conspicuous for his un-English clothes and, during the
performance of the symphony, for his extravagant gestures
signifying amazement and disapproval. Amid a welter of
discords the music comes to an end. The foreign critic
leaps to his feet, gesticulating: "Symphony? Sim fonny!"

Or: a variety show is in progress. An acrobat is balancing
on various objects starting with large beach-balls and continuing w**h ever smaller spheres, such as footballs,
melons, grapefruit, oranges. Finally to the accompan-
iment of a side-drum roll he balances on a crab-apple.
Member of audience (enthusiastic but not entirely satisfied): "Encore! On core!"

Sergeant Watkins and Captain Jones very occasionally
went on short day-passes to see Dylan, who in the autumn
of 1942 had found a place for himself and Caitlin to live in,
in 3 Wentworth Studios, Manresa Road, Chelsea. The
blitz was over, and bad air-raids did not begin again until
early in 1944. In *My Friend Dylan Thomas* Dr. Jones has
described these war-time meetings:

> I would have been wise not to seek Dylan out at all during
> those short leaves from Bletchley. It was impossible to
> detach him from a new circle of acquaintances some of whom
> treated me with less than courtesy . . .

At the same time, Dylan himself seemed different. He was now a famous man and often the centre of an admiring circle. I am ready to admit that in my feelings towards the closest of the sycophants there may have been a tinge of jealousy as I awkwardly shuffled about on the periphery of that charmed circle, but far stronger than this was the sense that Dylan had become remote. I suspect that if some proportion of the small amount of time I had for each London visit could have been spent alone with Dylan or with Dylan and two or three really close friends, any impression made on him by the insinuations of his new acquaintances would have vanished, and my feeling of the distance between us would have vanished too.

At least once he was able to see Dylan alone with Vernon and Phil Lindsay. Vernon describes the occasion thus:

. . . much of the time with them was spent doing composite poems to which each of us contributed a line. Dylan sometimes cheated and had more than one. Dan was a more lenient umpire and once, when I was not there, Dylan made a whole tiny poem for a child which ended 'And a little cruet flying in a cloud of jam'.

Vernon encountered the same fencing-in of Dylan, but, curiously enough for one who could be both arrogant and hot-tempered, he seemed content to wait about on the fringes of the crowd in the hope of, perhaps, walking home with Dylan afterwards, or, at the very least, managing to have a few words about poetry before rushing to Euston to get the last train back to Bletchley. He would endure, too, the frequent manifestation of a habit of Dylan's which greatly embarrassed him; Dylan would walk up to the tallest man in uniform in the pub and insult him, his country and the war so grossly that almost inevitably a fight developed. (John Prichard told me that he had once been walking past the Eight Bells when the door opened and Dylan came rolling out, followed by Caitlin, who said despairingly, "If only Dylan would just once pick on a *little* man!")

Dylan's attacks on uniform were awkward for Vernon, who as an NCO was not allowed to wear civilian clothes on short leave passes. Fortunately his sergeant's uniform did not annoy Dylan as much as Captain Jones's officer's dress, which maddened him; but he never knew whether he was expected to go to Dylan's aid in the fights, which his sense of justice told him were entirely Dylan's fault. He tried to excuse this by calling Dylan "the most aggressive pacifist I have ever seen" who "resented the smug talk he heard about the war, and . . . did not disguise his resentment." It was not always necessary to resort to insult or violence, either. Once Dylan confronted a man who was making slightly anti-Semitic remarks, and put on an act which culminated in his sinking his head on the bar, his shoulders heaving with sobs. "How could you!" cried Caitlin reproachfully to the appalled offender. "Don't you know Dylan and I are both Jews—red-headed Jews?"

As Dr. Jones had pointed out, "Dylan . . . welcomed hostile confrontations with strong or influential people"; sometimes these confrontations were for ethical reasons, sometimes for no reason at all but Dylan's personal dislike or even because of a personal tantrum. But after Dylan's death, Vernon persuaded himself that there was always a motive, and a good one, for such attacks. In a short piece in *Encounter* in 1956, he wrote:

> The poet of apparently destructive force was certainly the most ethical, the most constant of companions. He did not believe there was such a thing as a comfortable conscience. Where he found that the people around him were becoming puppets of self-satisfaction he did frequently break up the ground on which they stood. Such moods of violent exasperation coloured the false impression of a romantic poet rather than a true apprehension of the ethical witness. For a witness he always was, and the severest witness of his own behaviour. He tried to adapt his behaviour to his company. Considering each person to be an entire world, he was willing to go a long way with any man in his imagination to explore that world; but a world where Mammon took the place of God never failed to bore and disgust him. His instinct in conversation was to give, and to give prodigiously, and it was also to draw out ideas, to expose fallacies . . .

Dylan was not only courageous in attacking, if attack he must, the strongest and most formidable man in any company, he was also brave in air-raids; his courage was the true courage of the terror-stricken:

> He hated being in his house if there were an air raid, but he did not mind the raid if he were in a pub. That is to say, he minded it terribly, but he felt he was in the right place.

Vernon was staying at Manresa Road in early 1943 when a very bad raid began just as they had come back from the pub. They crouched under the big round table shown in the photograph opposite page 210 in the FitzGibbon biography, but Dylan was trembling so violently that the table shook. Vernon, to calm him, began talking of his belief in immortality, and Dylan, still trembling, made a reply which Vernon never forgot:

> In London, when the blinds were drawn
> Blackening a barbarous sky,
> He plucked, beneath the accusing beams,
> The mote out of his eye.
> In the one death his eye discerned
> The death all deaths must die.
>
> 'My immortality', he said,
> 'Now matters to my soul
> Less than the deaths of others . . .'
>
> — — —
>
> Not by the wars of human minds
> Nor by the jealous word
> Nor by the black of London's blinds
> Or coffin's rattling cord,
> But by the stillness of that voice
> The picture is restored.

'The death all deaths must die' is of course a reference to the line 'After the first death, there is no other', in *A Refusal to Mourn the Death by Fire of a Child in London*. This magnificent poem was sent to Vernon in the same envelope as *The Conversation of Prayer* and *A Winter's Tale*.

Another blitz incident was the basis for a sentence later to be used by Dylan in a number of ways. Dylan, on a visit to London from either Llangain or New Quay, was riding in a taxi down Regent Street with Vernon, when a V2 cut off its engine apparently directly overhead. (Connoisseurs of the V1 and V2 will remember that, if the V1 cut out directly overhead, you breathed a sigh of relief and horror, because it then glided on and exploded some distance away; but if a V2 cut out overhead, although you had time to breathe several sighs, they would almost certainly be your last). This particular rocket, however, came to earth some distance away, and as the taxi drove on through the dust and smoke Dylan said trembling, ''Wasn't it funny? I was sure we were going to be killed, and all I could think of was that I hoped I'd be blown to bits, because I couldn't bear the thought of my body being found with a copy of *Reveille* open at the pin-ups page.'' ''I should have been all right'', Vernon answered seriously, ''because I always carry Kierkegaard in my pocket.''

Dylan was very much amused, and Vernon's innocent remark turned up years later in *A Visit to America:*

> Of the lecture he [the visiting poet] remembers little but the applause and maybe two questions: 'Is it true that the young English intellectuals are *really* psychological?' or 'I always carry Kierkegaard in my pocket. What do you carry?'

In his edition of Dylan's letters Vernon says that he lost all the letters that came between August 1941 and July 1944. But he points out that

> The years, in fact, which are not here represented by letters, were years when we saw each other more often than at any time since he left Swansea. The letters that came then were often mere notes arranging to meet, the discussion of poems being postponed until the meeting, when the exact analysis of his written self-criticism gave way to the concise and lightning judgments of his conversation.

Besides the ''mere arrangements to meet'' Vernon says that

"some which were of extraordinary interest and some which were very funny disappeared. There was one describing his reactions to mine which were unforgettably comic.

But, as Vernon himself admitted, "Memory plays tricks with imagination and imagination with memory." From many conversations with him, I am inclined to think that, apart from the two letters he mentions above and "a long one of great interest", (which I believe to be the *Newly-Discovered Letter* printed in the *Anglo-Welsh Review* in 1972, and which had worked its way under the stiffened inner lining of Vernon's old R.A.F. kitbag) very few, if any, letters of importance were lost. Indeed, I am amazed that even the "arrangements to meet" did not survive, since Vernon was constitutionally unable to throw away a concert programme, a dentist's appointment card or even a bus-ticket. I can only think that his landlady in New Bradwell must occasionally have used her own discretion about the ever-accumulating mounds of paper in his room.

But after the war, in 1955, one letter, as Vernon discreetly puts it, "disappeared". He was giving a talk on Dylan, and afterwards—somewhat unwisely, as I could not help thinking at the time—he spread out all the letters on a small table for those who were interested to inspect. Still, the audience was a professional one whom he had every reason to trust, since some were friends and the others their colleagues. All the same . . . when we arrived home and I checked the letters, a single sheet with a draft of *There Was a Saviour* was missing, together with the "short one, almost entirely personal" which is referred to in the Introduction to the *Letters*, and which will be dealt with in the next chapter.

CHAPTER NINE: DICHOTOMIES

I cannot tell what shadows from the bough
Are truthful . . . —V. W.

On the 27th of July, 1944, Dylan wrote to Vernon, "I didn't think it was so long since we saw each other, or since I wrote to you . . ." and ending, "Write very soon, please, & tell me everything."

"Everything" included the fact that Vernon was engaged and wanted Dylan to be best man at his wedding in October. Dylan immediately answered with a short, very beautiful prose poem beginning "May all the bells of heaven ring their wildest for you both", praising marriage and calling down blessings from the past and the present on his friend. Vernon treasured this message, and its disappearance was a great blow to him; though of course the fact that it has no superscription and was written on a single sheet, smaller than a postcard, made it eminently suitable for "disappearing".

In the Sergeants' Mess at Bletchley (I was a Sergeant and Vernon a Flight-Sergeant, not through merit but because all Code-and-Cypher personnel were made senior NCOs, much to the fury of the camp personnel, who had to earn their promotions) one morning in September Vernon showed me a letter from Dylan with an enclosure. This was, "a month and a bit premature", the birthday poem for 1944, *Poem in October*, which had begun by being a birthday poem for 1941 with the first line

It was my twenty-seventh year to heaven.

Even in the Sergeants' Mess, among the smells of wartime coffee and wartime cigarettes, and the sounds of billiard and table-tennis balls knocking and bouncing, it was a staggeringly beautiful poem. And in the autumn evenings we sat on the grass by the pond and Vernon read aloud, sometimes from Yeats, once the entire Book of Job (a rather curious choice for a bridegroom, perhaps?) but most often poems and prose of Dylan's. I didn't (and don't) care much for the early poems, although some lines are memorable, or beautiful, or both; but the poems from *The Map of Love* are a very different matter. Vernon read aloud, too, all the stories from *Portrait of the Artist*, which were new to me.

A generation which has come to accept Dylan Thomas as a great poet, certainly, but a poet in text books, or examination syllabuses, a poet that students are expected to know, must find it difficult to understand the freshness, the explosive originality of his prose, and the majesty and exaltation of his poetry after the political and sociological poetry of the thirties. My student friends from Oxford asked me unbelievingly if I was really going to marry a man who knew Dylan Thomas, and I was proud to answer that Dylan Thomas was, in fact, to be best man at my wedding. The resultant clamour for invitations meant that I had to restrict the guests to family only. I had heard of Dylan's reputation for not keeping appointments, but Vernon assured me that the stories about his unreliability were apocryphal or, at least, exaggerated; and that in any case Dylan would never let him down. And Dylan himself had written ''. . . of course we are coming to your marriage, in our brightest colours''.

I was very glad indeed, afterwards, that I had resisted all the pleas for invitations, and had even kept secret the date and place of the wedding. I should, I think, have felt humiliated at being able to provide nothing but a wedding for a crowd who had really come to see a celebrity. In the event I hardly noticed that Dylan had not turned up until it was too late to matter: I had problems of my own.

Vernon and I were able only to get a 48-hour leave pass at the same time. The wedding was to be at two o'clock on October 2nd at St. Bartholomew the Great, and we were to have lunch in a private room at the Charing Cross Hotel with my parents, Vernon's two sisters, and Dylan. At about eleven o'clock we were walking down Regent Street, Vernon carrying a dozen long-stemmed golden roses for the altar of the church, when we ran into a friend from Bletchley, also on leave. "You look as though you're going to a wedding", he said. "We are", replied Vernon. "Would you like to come?" Not realising that it was Vernon's own wedding he was being invited to, and ready, as we all were in wartime, for any unexpected party or celebration, the friend happily agreed to turn up at St. Bartholomew the Great that afternoon, little knowing that he was to deputize at short notice for Dylan Thomas.

The question of the best man seemed to me to be Vernon's affair but the unexpected aunt waiting agog in a blue and pink velvet hat at the Charing Cross Hotel was indisputably mine. I had numerous aunts, uncles and cousins, and the impossibility of inviting them all to London, where the rocket-bombs fell at regular intervals, made me decide to tell them about my wedding only at the last moment. I had not counted on one intrepid aunt, on receipt of her letter, catching a train from bombed Birmingham to bombed London by the skin of her teeth; and I knew that no other aunt would ever believe that she had not been given advance information and was therefore an aunt favoured over all other aunts. I forsaw that this would lead to fearful inter-auntly warfare, but that no matter how much the aunts fought among themselves, they would all turn on me as one aunt. (In this I was absolutely right; the tumult and the shouting were still reverberating years after the wedding, and echoes of them floated about until the last aunt died.) But all I felt when Dylan had not turned up at the beginning of lunch was relief, since the velvet-hatted aunt, now abashed and inclined to be tearful after being made aware by my parents of the enormity of her behaviour, could have his vacant chair and his uneaten lunch.

Vernon, increasingly nervous, was reassured by a telephone call from a secretary at Gryphon Films (who, the Charing Cross Hotel porter said, had telephoned once or twice during the morning.) The secretary said that Mr. Thomas was *at that moment*—this was about one o'clock —in a taxi en route for the hotel. Vernon carefully directed that a plate and some beer should be put aside for the best man, and finished his own lunch in good spirits. But when two o'clock had arrived and Dylan had not, his anxiety became evident. He professed to feel sure that Dylan had gone straight to the church, but when I went upstairs to change, I passed him at the reception desk leaving complicated messages for Dylan in the event of his arriving after we had left.

The church of St. Bartholomew the Great lay open to the mellow autumn sky; only the Lady Chapel with the golden roses on the altar still had a roof. We waited there until the clergyman hinted that he had another wedding soon and could wait no longer. The old music-hall song went through my mind:

> There was I, waiting at the church,
> Waiting at the church;
> When I found he'd left me in the lurch,
> Lor, how it did upset me!

It did upset Vernon; it left a sore place in his heart that was not healed until Dylan's letter of excuse arrived nearly a month later. The Bletchley friend, hardly recovered from his amazement at the discovery that Vernon, one of Nature's bachelors, was to be married, was shoved up to the altar-rail in spite of his muted cries that he didn't know what a best man had to do, that he had never read the Marriage-service, that he himself had been married in a registry-office, that he would do everything wrong and then Vernon wouldn't be really married . . .

When the service was over and we came out into the autumn sunshine, Vernon looked hopefully round; and back at the hotel, and at the station. It was not until the train pulled out of St. Pancras that he said, ''That's the end of Dylan as far as I'm concerned.'' I tried to make excuses; Dylan might be ill, or his taxi might have broken down— any one of a dozen things might have happened. But Vernon would hear none of them. ''The only possible excuse'', he said bitterly, ''is that he's paralysed from the neck down, or dead.''

Nevertheless he waited anxiously for a letter from Dylan. When none came, I suggested that he might write or telephone himself. But this he absolutely refused to do. He must have thought that if Dylan cared so little about him that he could neither take the trouble to come to his wedding nor even apologise for not having done so, there could be little point in pretending any longer that they were friends. It was a bitter blow to him.

Nevertheless, when Dylan's letter did arrive, on the 30th October, all bitterness disappeared instantly. ''You see'', he said triumphantly, ''it wasn't his fault at all. He couldn't help it—there was nothing he could do.'' It was so evidently a relief to him to believe so, that I didn't mention my own misgivings. The letter seemed spurious to me: it sounded guilty, but not guilty about the things it apologised for. Besides, there was that telephone call to the Charing Cross Hotel saying that Dylan was already in the taxi. And if he had forgotten the name of the church, why not either drive to or telephone the hotel to ask the name? Or failing that, why not simply go to the hotel and wait for the wedding party to come back from the church? Or why not at least have telephoned Vernon's sister, whose number was in the Directory? There were too many unanswered, and for me unanswerable, questions. Vernon was happy, but I could not help feeling mistrustful. Years later Paul Ferris, who was then researching for his biography, told me that Dylan had been in the office of a London publisher, David Gottlieb, in the early afternoon of October 2nd, being paid £10 of a £50 advance on a projected work (which, incidentally, was never written). I wondered again what had really happened. We know that Dylan had been to Gryphon Films and had been put into the taxi which had been directed to the Charing Cross Hotel before one o'clock. In an article for the *Anglo-Welsh Review* in 1972, I wrote (and believed), ''The unfamiliar was always terrible to him. Sometimes, fortified by drink or supported by friends, he could nerve himself to face it, but at other times he could only retreat. The real reason why he did not turn up at our wedding was, I am sure, that

he could not face meeting people he didn't know . . .''. I
don't now believe that. I don't know why he didn't turn
up. If he had stopped the taxi for a pre-lunch drink, and just
not stopped drinking till the pubs closed—that I could
understand. ''Procrastination is an element in which I
live'', he wrote, and he procrastinated often enough to his
own disadvantage. But he did leave the pub, and pretty
soon: to get some money, and he didn't stay long in the
publisher's. So why couldn't he have spared a few moments to wish Vernon well? If he knew anything at all about
Vernon, he knew what pain he would be inflicting by not
turning up. So did he know anything about Vernon? If he
did, did he care what he was doing? Did he just not think
about it at all, or did he think he could explain everything
away afterwards?

By the time I knew Dylan well enough to ask him these
questions, I also knew that whatever he might say in
answer, it would not be the truth. As Dr. Jones has said,
''Dylan prided himself on preferring the lie to the truth'';
but also, if you tell lies often enough, you begin to forget
what the truth is. I suppose if I had asked Dylan why he
didn't come to the wedding, or the hotel, or the station, I
might have had a dozen answers: one of them might have
been true, but Dylan would no longer have known which it
was.

So when I first met Dylan, at the beginning of
December, there was already, in spite of my admiration for
his poems and stories, a shadow between us. It was in the
back bar of the Café Royal, and Dylan, who had promised
to be waiting there, ''henna'd, camelia'd, & smelling of
moths'', was not there when we arrived, nor did he come
until some time later. There was a real reason this time: he
had been seeing Caitlin off at Waterloo, and had put her
luggage, including handbag with tickets and money, on
the wrong train which had moved out before the things
could be snatched away. Caitlin had been furious, and
there had been explaining and telephoning and borrowing
to be done before she could go.

Dylan arrived in the Café Royal hot and very evidently

wishing he hadn't arranged the meeting at all. To do him justice, he did his best to be pleasant, but he was not used to concealing his emotions. He told funny stories, he showed off, he blustered about his wife and children, he stopped passing friends and had confidential chats with them, he dropped names, drinks and cigarette ash. After an hour of this I could no longer hide from myself that what I felt at my first meeting with the poet of *Holy Spring* and *Poem in October* was, inescapably, boredom. I was bored with his behaviour and with what he was saying: I wanted out.

With a few exceptions, the times when I met Dylan always made me feel like that: the time in the Eight Bells when Caitlin was deliberately flirting with an Air Force officer to make Dylan jealous, and succeeded; the time when Caitlin was rude to the waiter in a Chinese restaurant and Dylan was rude to Caitlin; the time when we went to the pictures and Dylan and Caitlin quarrelled in barely subdued voices as to whether we should go because the film was so bad or stay because it was so bad; the time in the Boar's Head, Carmarthen, when we were asked to leave because Llewelyn was running among the crowded tables, chanting and knocking glasses and elbows. And oh, the pubs, the "gabbling drink-grey crush", the smoke, the boozy wit that seemed witty only to the boozers!

But there were exceptions: Dylan reading the draft for *August Bank Holiday* and asking nervously at the end, "Do you think it's any good, really?"; Dylan lying on the grass at Pennard and talking about Dickens; Dylan playing Statues with Dan and Vernon in the evening light; Dylan in Swansea looking at the bomb-sites, wet-cheeked with cold and grief, saying "Where we used to go is nowhere at all now". And Dylan saying to me, "You think I'm not a serious person: but I am. I have to be serious to write my kind of poems". These, and a few other occasions, showed me what I thought of as the "real" Dylan, who was always there under the masks. But it became increasingly difficult to find him, and the masks took on a reality of their own.

"The war, they say," wrote Dylan to Oscar Williams in

March 1945, "is all over bar the dying." On the same day
he wrote to Vernon about an incident in which a Com-
mando captain (subsequently tried for, and acquitted of,
attempted murder) fired off a sub-machine gun in wood-
and-asbestos Majoda, Dylan's rented bungalow in New
Quay.* The description ended, "At debt's and death's door
I now stand with a revolving stomach, waiting for V.1000
and the Bubonic Plague." It was the logical outcome of all
Dylan's taunts and needlings of service men, and it terrified him. As far as I know, however bad his subsequent
behaviour in pubs and out of them, he never again challenged anybody to a fight.

The incident terrified Vernon too. All his friends except
David Lewis, Wyn's younger brother, had come safely
through the war; and in spite of Dylan's romantic threats of
a young death, Vernon saw himself and Dylan as growing
old like Yeats, writing poems "moving, like Swedenborg's
angels, towards the dayspring of their youth". He had
never really imagined living in a world without Dylan. He
wrote to Francis in May:

> I've heard twice lately from Dylan, who was involved in a
> dangerous incident a month or so ago . . . It's a very lucky
> thing that no life was lost. I loathe fights, and simply don't
> understand why Dylan has them, but he's very sorry about it
> all, & says he wasn't provocative at all that evening.

It was in a postscript to the machine-gun letter that
Dylan asked Vernon, with great urgency, to write a "personal introduction" for a book of his Selected Writings to
be brought out in America:

> To me, of course, that introduction coming from you, as my
> friend and as—we've both said this, with a kind of giggling
> gravity—the only other poet except me whose work I really
> like today—would be the best in the world. Let me know if
> you would do it; and, if you would, could you do it *terribly*
> quickly and let me have it so that I can send it off almost at
> once. It's a lot to ask, and you hardly ever write prose, but . . .

*A full account of this incident is given in Paul Ferris's *Dylan Thomas*,
Chapter 8.

Well, I'll hear from you. We know each other by doing so many things together, from croquet to bathing (me for the first time) in the icy moon, poetry and very high teas, getting drunk, reading, reading, reading, sea staring, Swansea, Gower, Laugharne, London . . . I've written thousands of letters to you; if you've kept some you could use what you liked to help build up this "human portrait" of this fat pleader.

An introduction from Vernon might be "the best in the world" for Dylan, but Vernon was not the first person he had asked to write it. Donald Taylor had been staying in New Quay in March, and Dylan must have asked him to do an introduction too, because there was a reminder in a letter to Taylor on March 27th, the day before he wrote to Vernon, "Please don't forget to have a shot at doing those 'personal' thousand words for the introduction to my American *Selected Writing*. Let me see what you bang out. If you're too busy, I can ask Tommy Earp to do something but I hope you aren't."

It looks as though Dylan was asking several of his friends to have a go at the introduction, intending to choose the best to send to New Directions.

If Vernon had known that Dylan was asking other friends, he would not have tried to write the piece. He did try, and it worried him very much. He sat among the Victorian plush of our landlady's little parlour in Stony Stratford, writing and crossing out, and writing and crossing out. "I can't write about my closest friend", he said. He sat up nearly all night writing the thousand words, and typed them before breakfast so that they would catch the first post. "But he won't like it", he said. "I know he won't like it."

Dylan wrote politely:

It was so good of you to write that little personal—what?— thing, then, so quickly and so very nicely. Just, I should imagine, what New Directions want, and I have sent it off *just* as it is, not even altering 'good' to 'great' or putting in a paragraph about my singing voice or horsemanship. Thank you a lot. It did, I know, sound rather awful: Write about me.

If you had asked me to do it about you, I think I should have pleaded everything from writer's cramp to never having met you except in the dark, & then only once.

But Vernon was despondent. "It wasn't what he wanted", he said. "I've let him down. I knew he wouldn't like it". In a note to the *Letters* he wrote, years afterwards:

> The American edition of . . . *Selected Writings* . . . did not afterwards use a personal note. I did write one . . . but I did not, so far as I can remember, quote from any of his letters. Nor was the note at all adequate or satisfactory, for what one is asked to do is never either, unless it is done without embarrassment. My own embarrassment was acute, like that of a man holding a many-coloured kite on a windless day.

Whether rightly or wrongly, he felt that what he had written had displeased Dylan in some way—perhaps it was not admiring enough, or as admiring as Dylan thought it ought to be. He heard nothing of Dylan between May 1945 and April 1946. *Deaths and Entrances* was published in February 1946, and was the first of Dylan's books of which a copy, affectionately inscribed, was not sent to Vernon. He bought, as I remember, at least two dozen copies and sent them to all his friends. "Its poems are wonderful, and the best he has written", he wrote to Francis, ". . . he's not much of a correspondent—to me, anyway, though he used to be." And again:

> I'm glad you are making good use of your translation of Dylan's 'A Prospect of the Sea'. He seems to have deserted me now that he is permanently in London [Dylan was in fact living in Oxford at this time] but if he does come to Swansea I'll be glad to see him. His book has been very well received and they are certainly the most beautiful lyrical poems he has written. I do not like the very occasional word-tricks, 'once below a time', 'happy as the heart was long', because I do not think they are poetry or even Dylan Thomas, but Joyce's ghost walking. But they are tiny blemishes in grand and lovely work.

He bought every newspaper, magazine and periodical in case there should be a review of *Deaths and Entrances*: and used to say, after Dylan's death, in talks all over England, Wales and America, that Herbert Read was the sole reviewer to say the only possible thing about the book, ''These poems cannot be reviewed; they can only be acclaimed.''

Vernon had seen all, and helped with some, of the poems in *Deaths and Entrances*, except *Fern Hill*, and was thus very closely involved with them. Although he held to his own view that no poet should ever review the work of another living poet, he lost no opportunity of proclaiming, in lectures and poetry-readings, his belief that they were great poetry:

> Out of the dust of bombed London he raised the victims of tragedy to their own dignity and the glory which he, as a religious witness, acclaimed. Such poems are *A Refusal to Mourn the Death, by Fire, of a Child in London*, and *Ceremony after a Fire Raid*. In others, like *Fern Hill* and *Poem in October* the praise of life is unfolded, in stanzas of vivid colour and a compelling, assonantal music, through a re-creation of his own boyhood.

He had at first had doubts over the stanza form of *Vision and Prayer*:

> in which the verses of the first part formed the shape of a diamond and the verses of the second part the shape of an hour-glass . . . The device was one that George Herbert had used, a poet whom Dylan particularly loved and admired. Yet the poem had found its original spur in the work of a very different poet. Dylan told me, when he was just beginning to write it, that he had read a most wonderful statement of Rilke about God being born in the next room. This must, I think, have been the poem *Du Nachbar Gott* from the Stundenbuch. . .
>
> *Vision and Prayer* was rightly acclaimed as a fine religious poem. I had suggested to him that, although the words of the first part appeared to fit the diamond-pattern organically, there were verses in the second part where the words seemed to have been drilled into position to fit the pattern of the prayer-wheel and the line-endings did not coincide with the pauses of the voice, as they do, for instance, in Herbert's *Easter Wings*. So I wondered whether he would consider trying out the second part in verses with lines of equal length.

The suggestion did not appeal to Dylan at all. He had chipped out his poem with consummate care, working on it for months like an old carpenter, and he did not want to change it. He was right to stick to the pattern in which the poem was conceived, and I do not see now how he could have changed it without writing a different poem.

Vernon made a suggestion about *Poem in October* which met with more success:

> He did alter 'bare' to 'winged' trees in the second stanza and 'brown with October blood' (which was my only criticism) to 'leaved with October blood' in the last. It was the most beautiful poem he had made, and one of the most beautiful, I think, in the language.

Dylan bore with suggestions very amiably. I remember suggesting to him myself, after seeing *A Refusal to Mourn* in manuscript, that instead of "Deep with the first dead lies London's daughter" he might have varied the alliteration by writing

> Low with the first dead lies London's daughter.

He looked at me for a few seconds with great intensity, and then said, "Oh, I do wish I had thought of that." Of course he had thought of, and rejected, it; but he made me (who knew less than nothing about the writing of poems) feel gratified and proud. It was the "real" Dylan at his most amiable.

In a talk which Vernon gave at Attingham Park, he analysed the reasons why he thought *Deaths and Entrances* not only great but unique:

> First, there is a particular way in which Dylan uses language as an instrument to stir the imagination. Word-play and puns are used as a creative element, and colloquialisms are made dynamic by their context. Phrases that hit the ear with one meaning are found, on examination, to have a second and deeper meaning.
>
> Second, the religious base of his poems is organic and consistent. When asked to describe his poems and what they meant to him, Dylan called them 'Statements on the way to the Grave'.

Third, the images of birds, creatures, fruit, and all living things are seen from the point of view of their Creator, from the Book of Genesis.

Fourth, pattern-making and symmetry are a strong element in the structure of these poems. The demands of exact pattern are very seldom neglected.

Vernon had of course, in spite of Dylan's long silence, written to him on the publication of *Deaths and Entrances*, but Dylan did not reply. Perhaps he did not get the letter: he had been moving about from friend to relation until he came to rest at Holywell Ford in Oxford in March 1946. By then Vernon had been demobilized for two months and was back in Swansea.

CHAPTER TEN: A SINGLE VOICE

So dear to thought are these remembered things. —V.W.

Vernon's second book, *The Lamp and the Veil*, was published while he was still in uniform, late in 1945. The reviews ranged from *The Listener's* "Nothing comparable has been published since *Little Gidding*" to *Time and Tide's* "How that Mr. Watkins does go on." But from the critic for whom Vernon cared most there came no word, not even a letter of thanks for the book which had of course been sent to him before publication. It was the more disappointing since in two of the three long poems of which the book consisted Dylan made a personal appearance. Walter Allen, in *Time and Tide*, not only reviewed *The Lamp and the Veil* with *Deaths and Entrances* but also quoted the verse from *Yeats in Dublin* in which

> An image stands on Carmarthen sands
> With the black birds overhead.

Yet he made no connection; not a single critic connected this "image" and the "extravagant hero of night" with Dylan Thomas.

To say that Vernon was hurt at Dylan's silence is to trivialise his feelings. He loved Dylan unconditionally, and therefore expected nothing in return; but he had rushed home from Ireland to Laugharne with his first draft of the Yeats poem, and had worked on subsequent versions with Dylan's help; and the other two poems were about their own blitzed Swansea. The last poem, *The Broken Sea*, was dedicated to Francis Dufau-Labeyrie's daughter, Vernon's god-child, born in Paris in 1940, and was in part a celebration of the shared past of those three young men,

> All the villainies of the fire-and-brimstone-visited town.

Everywhere there were small reminders to and of Dylan:

> . . . the glow-lamped Eumenides' house; . . .
> The world of a child's one town . . .
> Between Cwmdonkin railing and black-faced Inkerman
> > Street"

and a reference to Dylan's own poem *There Was a Saviour*:

> But the crust breaks in Christ's original radium.

It would have meant a great deal to him to know that Dylan noticed and cared for these things. Perhaps he did; but he did not find time to tell Vernon so. Vernon wrote sadly to Francis in 1946, "I'm glad you are making good use of your translation of Dylan's *A Prospect of the Sea*. He seems to have deserted me now that he is permanently in London . . .''

Dylan was not in fact in London, but in Oxford, living in "a converted telephone-kiosk, with a bed where the ledge for directories used to be." In April 1946 the long silence was broken; Dylan wrote:

> There's never been such a long time between our letters, and I hope, atom willing, there won't be again . . . It's been my fault, of course, that goes without whining . . .

His reason for writing was to borrow Vernon's essay on Wilfred Owen, since he himself was about to do an Owen programme for the B.B.C. He promised to return the essay "spotlessly unAeronwied", but it could not be found. "Have you", the letter continued,

> a little sheetless, must be sheetless, dogbox with nails for me to sleep in? Any shelter for a night? . . . Then we could, maybe, all spend one evening together, wipey-eyed, remembering, locked in these damned days, the as-then-still-forgiven past.

We were at that time living in the Uplands of Swansea, at the top of Glanmor Hill, a few minutes from Cwmdonkin Park. But Dylan on his visit had no wish to revisit any scenes of his youth. He was writing the August Bank Holiday radio script, and he wanted to read it aloud, hear our criticisms, discuss it, and then go out to the pub. It was the first time I had heard him read his own work. For the first few minutes it seemed to me mannered and artificial; after that, and for ever after, it seemed the only way to read Dylan Thomas.

In the bitter winter of February 1947 Dylan was in Swansea again, gathering material for *Return Journey*. He and Vernon walked about the snow-covered ruins of their past, and it seemed for a short time as though the old relationship had been restored.

In March Vernon wrote to tell Dylan that *Ballad of the Mari Lwyd* was being broadcast on the Third Programme. He received the answer,

> I'm looking forward to hearing 'Mari Lwyd' on Thursday. I'm one of the readers. I hope you won't mind too much.

Dylan must, at their last meeting, have been already aware that he was scheduled to take part in the *Ballad*, and Vernon thought it strange that he had not said so: but he was delighted that it was so. And indeed Dylan was a superb Leader of the Dead. It is nothing less than a tragedy that the B.B.C. should have destroyed all records of this magnificent performance. Of course Vernon wrote a letter of praise and pleasure, but no answer came from Dylan. (If Vernon's letters to Dylan had been preserved, it would be seen that he wrote two or three to every one of Dylan's.) But now that he had become conscious of the change in Dylan's feeling for him, the old spontaneity was lost. If a letter remained unanswered, Vernon did not break the silence, however long it might be.

But in April 1948, more than a year after the *Mari Lwyd* broadcast, Patric Dickinson asked Vernon to compile one of his *Time for Verse* programmes on the B.B.C. Home Service. These consisted of half-an-hour of poetry, often on a single theme. Vernon chose poems about old age. He was to read the prose commentary, and he asked for Dylan and V.C. Clinton-Baddeley as readers of the verse. Clinton-Baddeley had a deep musical voice, and had been trained as a verse-reader by Yeats himself.

Vernon had strong views on the reading of poetry, and

especially disliked dramatic reading. He said that actors
were usually thinking of themselves, while a verse-reader
must think only of the words he was reading. To his mind,
a poem should be read with as much care as a musical
score; just as a musician would not dream of ignoring a
rest, or play a crotchet as a minim, no more should a verse-
reader ignore the end of a line or a verse, so that the poem
sounded like prose. He was fond of quoting William
Morris, who is said to have left a reading of his poems saying morosely, "It took me a damned long time to get that
into verse." Both the rhythm and the tempo of a poem
should be clearly perceptible to the trained or the intuitive
ear.

But his greatest condemnation was reserved for those
who read poems "with expression". He felt that the poet
had taken very great trouble to select the words which
most exactly conveyed the impression or the feeling he
wished to present. All the reader had to do was to say the
words with the correct rhythm; if he too added emotion,
the transmission would be overloaded or confused. This
was another reason why he disliked actors reading; they
had been trained to a different technique, and could rarely
leave the poem alone to do its own work. He set out his
own theories in a reading at Stratford-on-Avon in 1958:

> I was asked the other day what advantage it was to hear a poet
> read his own work. I answered, 'However badly he reads, he
> has one overwhelming advantage. He heard the poem first.'
> My questioner was not satisfied. 'Surely', he said, 'when a
> poet has written a poem, his work is done? He can then leave
> it to some-one else, to the best trained person, to interpret it.'
> He contended that a poet was a professional writer, but an
> amateur reader, and that a professional work demanded a pro-
> fessional interpretation. It seems to me that an actor is often
> too conscious of the audience and too little conscious of the
> poem. In satirical or dramatic verse an actor may excel, but in
> lyric poetry everything depends upon the discipline of the
> poem. No reader of lyric poetry will succeed who does not
> observe a monotonous base. I am easily misunderstood here.
> I do not mean, of course, that the whole of any lyric poem
> must be read on one note. I mean that the intensity of a poem is

more likely to be felt and kept if it is held down by the strictness of its pattern. That is why, though I have heard Tennyson splendidly read by different people, I have only once heard the exactnéss of rhythm which entirely communicated the poem, and that was in an old cylindrical recording of Tennyson reading himself. This brings me to my final point: whatever the duty of an actor is towards an audience, the poet's duty is very clear. He must not do more than reproduce the poem as he heard it at the final moment of composition.

Vernon was speaking here to an audience of teachers of verse-speaking, and many of them profoundly disagreed with him. In an address to the Poetry Society in 1966, he described the follow-up:

> I was thanked in a very kind letter and told that my way of reading, with a little adjustment, could be perfectly adapted to a poetry audience. Then the letter went into more detail, recommending expression and variations of pitch. I replied that I *could* read like that, but only did so when I was imitating . . . the way in which I hated to hear poetry read aloud.

Dylan and Vernon were pretty well agreed as to the way in which they liked poetry to be read, though Dylan was incomparably the better reader of the two, because of his magnificent voice and the fact that (however nervous he might be before a reading) he was in complete command of himself once he had begun. They both steadfastly refused invitations to judge verse-speaking competitions, having been warned by Dylan's experience in hearing a verse-speaking choir reciting *And Death Shall Have No Dominion*:

> Oh dear. Picked voices picking the rhythm to bits, chosen elocutionists choosing their own meanings, ten virgins weeping slowly over a quick line, matrons mooing the refrain, a conductor with all his vowels planed to the last e.

But Vernon had one advantage over Dylan in the reading of verse; although he played no instrument, he listened constantly to music, and his ear for variations of rhythm was extremely subtle. Dylan, as Dr. Daniel Jones has pointed out, was musically illiterate. Rhythm was not in fact an important element of poetry for him.

Dr. Jones is, so far as I know, the only critic who has pointed out that Dylan "never established in his mind the obvious connection between word-stress and musical accent"; Dylan's poetry was based almost entirely on quantitative rather than accentual metre,* that is, on the number of syllables in each line regardless of the stress. Of course he could write accentual verse; but when he did, how did he hear it?

It seems likely that he heard accentual verse as though it were syllabic. How else can one account for his failure, for it was no less, to read it? I heard him attempt to do so, and fail miserably, several times.

The first time was at the rehearsal of the *Old Age* programme. There was a little embarrassment when the two readers turned up, as they had not been speaking to each other for several months, and neither was aware that the other was to be his co-reader. But they shook hands civilly enough, with apologies and compliments equally insincere, and settled down to rehearse. Vernon began the commentary with an anonymous reference to Dylan:

> I once asked a friend if he would go to a party where all the guests were under eighteen, and he refused; but he added that if they had all been over eighty he would have gone.

Clinton-Baddeley read Shakespeare's *Crabbed Age and Youth*, after which Dylan was to read A. E. Housman's *Fancy's Knell*, with its beautiful verse

> Wenlock Edge was umbered,
> And bright was Abdon Burf,
> And warm between them slumbered
> The smooth green miles of turf;
> Until from grass and clover
> The upshot beam would fade,
> And England over
> Advanced the lofty shade.

---

*By quantitative metre I mean a metre in which the same number of syllables occur in each line: by accentual metre, a metre in which the stresses on certain syllables in every line conform to an accepted pattern.

in which the delicate rhythm of the seventh line is entirely dependent on its five syllables being spoken in exactly the same time as the six syllables of the all the other lines— just as, say, a minim and a crotchet in one bar of music must take the same time to play as the three crotchets in the next bar. Dylan could not see this; worse, he could not read the six-syllabled lines as accentual metre at all. The poem was ruined. At first, Vernon tried to make him see this, but without success. Then Clinton-Baddeley joined in (his own sense of rhythm was perfect) and this proved disastrous: from being flushed and petulant, Dylan was on the verge of a real tantrum. He had to be allowed to read the poem as he wanted to; at the suggestion that he might read the Shakespeare and Clinton-Baddeley the Housman he threatened to walk out. It was quite evident that he thought the others were ganging up on him, and that he could not see the point they were making.

He was still thoroughly ruffled when his turn came to read his own poem *Among Those Killed in the Dawn Raid was a Man Aged a Hundred.* He read the first two lines perfectly:

When the morning was walking over the war
He put on his clothes and stepped out and he died,

and then disaster struck. He could not manage the first half of the next line:

The locks yawned loose and a blast blew them wide,

though he tried again and again. He tried "the locks lawned loose"; he tried "the yocks yawned loose"; he tried "the yocks lawned loose"; really desperate now, he hurried over "the lawns locked loose" and the "yawns loosed locks". We all watched in fascinated horror as his face grew redder, the veins on his forehead pulsed faster, and the long-awaited tantrum arrived. He jumped up, hurled his book across the rehearsal room and bawling out, "Oh, God! I'd never have written the bloody line if I'd known it was going to be as hard as this to read!", he made for the door. He was, of course, soothed and comforted, and the live broadcast an hour later went off without incident; but the scene was unlike Dylan, who made slips of the tongue only when very drunk, and not often then. The virtuoso who could read Dai's Boast from *In Parenthesis* and Hopkins' *The Leaden Echo and the Golden Echo* without a single fluff was not likely to wreck half a line of one of his own poems unless something had happened to upset him. Although it seemed then (and seems now) unlikely that Dylan could not hear accentual metre when read by others, it was evident that he could not reproduce it himself.

I knew then why Dylan, although superb as Satan in *Paradise Lost*, yet created a feeling of unease in dialogue. It was because he was reading Milton in syllabic metre while everybody else in the programme was reading him in accentual metre. It would have been much better if he had read all the ten books himself.

This was not an isolated occasion. Dr. Jones has told the story of Dylan's trying, and failing, to write a poem to be sung to the Londonderry Air: "It was impossible to explain to Dylan why it does not follow that a phrase of music requiring ten syllables can be sung to *any* ten-syllable line." Roy Campbell, who handled many of Dylan's Third Programme readings, said that he had difficulty with "correct" poets like Pope and Dryden. And in another programme with Vernon the same problem arose. Dylan was reading three of Vernon's sea ballads, and Vernon spoke the prose commentary. They ran into trouble with the second poem, *Ballad of the Three Coins*, which begins:

> I know this road like the back of my hand
> From birth to the lonely sea
> With a windblown dog and a bottle of sand,
> And I count my curses three.

Dylan had never heard the idiom "like the back of my hand", and laid enormous emphasis on the nouns, thus making the line virtual nonsense: then he wiped the simple, strongly-accented ballad-rhythm out of existence by his weighty syllabic reading. But his voice and manner

were always magnificent, and the B.B.C.'s destruction of
these two programmes seems not only pointless, but, considering the income made by the Caedmon record company, very short-sighted.

Another programme in which Vernon and Dylan took
part, this time with Daniel Jones, Alfred Janes and John
Prichard, was a programme on the Welsh Home Service,
rather pretentiously called *Swansea and the Arts*; but it
was not at all pretentious in content. Five practising artists, three writers, a composer and a painter, all born or living in Swansea, talked about the town and its effect on
their work. It is interesting, too, because it is almost the
only public expression still on record of what Dylan
thought about Vernon:

> First of all, then, Vernon Watkins, poet and present. I think
> him to be the most profound and greatly accomplished
> Welshman writing poems in English, and he is one of the few
> poets I know, intensely occupied with his craft, who happily
> makes a living in a way that has nothing to do with words. So
> many writers, because their own serious writing does not
> pay, live by writing about writing, lecturing about writing,
> reviewing other writers, scriptwriting, advertising, journal-
> ising, boiling pots for the chainstore publishers; Vernon Wat-
> kins writes nothing but poems. Very properly, he makes his
> living by other people's money: in a bank. He is proof against
> the dangers (so tempting to poets, such as myself, who are
> not qualified to extract their livelihoods other than by the use
> of language) the dangers of mellifluous periphrasis, otiose
> solipsism, the too-easy spin and flow of the paid word.

Vernon and Dylan made one television appearance
together, in April 1953. Dr. Daniel Jones has described this
programme in *My Friend Dylan Thomas*, but for once his
encyclopaedic memory has let him down. The performers
consisted of himself, Dylan, Alfred Janes and Vernon (not
John Prichard). Wynford Vaughan-Thomas acted as a kind
of link-man. The scene was supposedly Janes's studio, and
his paintings, portraits of Dylan and Vernon, Swansea and
Gower landscapes, led to the 'bits' spoken by each part-
icipant. It was an interesting but not successful pro-

gramme. The paintings came out well, and Wynford Vaughan-Thomas and Daniel Jones seemed perfectly at ease, but the others were evidently not. Dylan particularly made a mess of his part; he first caught sight of himself on the monitor set and remained, eyes bulging and jaw dropping, speechless for several long seconds; then he repeated some of his sentences. It was not quite a disaster but it was (as Mr. Wodehouse might have said) very far from being an aster.

Vernon, however, refused to admit that Dylan wasn't very good in this programme. Years later, in 1961, the *Texas Quarterly* intended to publish a script of the programme, calling it *A Painter's Studio*, by Dylan Thomas.* Warren Roberts, the then Director of the Centre, sent Vernon a proof for his comments on his own part; but the comments, when they came, were largely concerned with Dylan:

> If the *Texas Quarterly* are going to print this piece I think it very important that there should be a preliminary note explaining that only a part of it is Dylan Thomas's own writing. There is all the difference in the world between one of Dylan's scripted programmes for radio, such as you find in *Quite Early One Morning*, and this, which is a sketch, done in conjunction with the producer David J. Thomas, for a television programme featuring Alfred Janes's portraits and sitters, which took place, unscripted, in April 1953.
> [Here follow some corrections of the proof.]
> Much more important than these small inaccuracies is the distinction which must be made between Dylan's actual writing, and the introductory passages, half suggested, half dictated and noted down while Dylan was obviously in conversation with either Wynford Vaughan-Thomas or D. J. Thomas or both. Dylan would never *write*:
> > any of the first page; (imagine him writing 'etc!')
> > any of the second, with the exception of the line: And Jones replies: 'About Daniel Jones.'
> The rest, with the exception of the final paragraph, is immensely good and authentic; and in actual rehearsal and

*This was based on notes in Dylan's own script, recently acquired by the Humanities Research Center.

production it only underwent small variations, because Dylan couldn't quite remember his words.

These programmes were often the only contacts between Dylan and Vernon during the years when Dylan's letters became infrequent.

Vernon's third book of poems *The Lady with the Unicorn* was published in October 1948. If Dylan did not buy it, he at least took the trouble to tell Vernon that he had bought it

> and left it, *at once,* in a cab. Before I had opened it . . . Now I must wait till Christmas to read you.

Of course Vernon immediately sent him another copy.

> "Lovely book", he replied . . . I am reading it from the beginning, some every night, slow & light & lifted . . . I'll write again when I've read all the (to me) new beautiful poems.

But (again of course) he did not write. Although he was to live another five years, this was the last letter Vernon received from him, with the exception of a note of a few lines after Vernon had written to him on the death of his father. There had been a time when no published poem of Vernon's would have been "new" to Dylan, but that time had gone, and Vernon made no attempt to bring it back.

Although there were no more letters, Dylan and Vernon did still, in the last years of his life, meet occasionally. Sometimes (but by no means always) when he was in Swansea he would drop in at the bank and he and Vernon would have a hurried lunch at the Bush Hotel, or go to a cricket-match for an hour. It was at one such cricket-match that Dylan first told Vernon and Dan Jones about the new piece he was writing which was later to be called *Under Milk Wood.* In its very early days, this was to be an account of a village which was so wicked (in an infantile way) that it was to be collectively tried by a jury consisting of delegates from other Welsh villages. As each inhabitant stammered or boasted about his sins, the jury was to roar out "Ach-y-fi!" in delighted horror.

One winter night Dylan was merely passing through

Swansea on his way to Laugharne, and Vernon telephoned me to say that he was going to have a quick drink at the station with him, and would be a little late for the evening meal. The evening passed away, and the last bus from Swansea to Pennard, just before midnight, had come and gone, with no sign of Vernon. I had gone to bed when, about one o'clock, an exhausted and dishevelled poet stumbled up to the front door. It appeared that the "quick drink" had gone on until the pubs closed, when Dylan, afraid of Caitlin's rage if he did not turn up that night, had found a taxi-driver willing to take him to Laugharne for the sum of forty pounds. "It seemed a reasonable price to us at the time", said Vernon feebly. He himself had arrived at Pennard on the last bus, but after walking along the cliff-top path, five minutes from the bus-stop, that led to his bungalow, "—walking for a long time", he assured me— he heard the sea booming close below him and felt the spray on his face. He had walked about a mile and a half to the foot of Pobbles Bay. "It was the fog that misled me", he said, "—such a thick fog." It had been an exceptionally clear and frosty night.

It was always Vernon who, busy though he was in the bank, had to make the effort to see Dylan. I remember only one occasion on which Dylan came to see Vernon. He had just come back from his first American tour, and Alfred Janes and his wife brought him and Caitlin to Pennard on a Saturday after lunch. It was a fresh and sunny day in June, the sea was glittering, the garden was full of roses. Ethel Ross and Dan Jones and his wife and son came later in the afternoon. It was, I should think, the last time until the day of Dylan's funeral that such a group of old Swansea friends was together.

We all started off along the cliffs to go down to the bay for a swim, but we had not been strolling for more than a few minutes when Dylan threw himself on the turf, panting. "I can't possibly walk any more", he said. "I'll wait here till you come up." I expected Vernon to stay with him, but Vernon was hot from the bank and wanted his bathe, so I felt, as hostess, I must stay. We went back to the

garden and sat on the lawn in the shade. I had never felt at
ease with Dylan but now, for about three-quarters of an
hour, I did. He had a glass of lager, and sipped it at long
intervals as he talked. He said how terrifying and fascin-
ating and boring he had found the Americans; how self-
conscious he felt about his teeth, and how, having found
out that the forty-six gleaming teeth every American possessed were often the result of artifice, not nature, he had
made enquiries about a few gleaming teeth for himself—
"just the front ones". But to have even the four front ones
crowned would have cost "hundreds and hundreds of dollars", he said, his eyes bulging at the thought of so much
money for four teeth. We talked about Dickens, whom we
both passionately loved, and he rolled over, squealing with
breathless laughter, when I quoted my favourite bits: Mrs.
Gamp's elegy for her children:

> 'My own', I says, 'has fallen out of three-pair backs, and had
> damp doorsteps settled on their lungs, and one was turned up
> smilin' in a bedstead unbeknown.'

Then we talked about Dickens' journalism, which Dylan
was not so familiar with as the novels, and I said I thought
his prose was more like that of Dickens than any other
modern writer—certainly more than that of J. B. Priestley
(often at that time alleged to be the Dickens of the twent-
ieth century). His *Memories of Christmas*, for example,
had some similarities of construction and theme to Dickens' *A Christmas Tree*; and *Return Journey* was based on
the same idea, that of the man tracing his boyhood and
childhood back through time, as Dickens' own contribution to *The Haunted House*; the lament at the end:

> No other ghost has haunted the boy's room, . . . than the
> ghost of my own childhood, the ghost of my own innocence,
> the ghost of my own airy belief. Many a time have I pursued
> the phantom—never with this man's stride of mine to come
> up with it, never with these man's hands of mine to touch it,
> never more to this man's heart of mine to hold it in its purity

is not unlike the famous ending of *Return Journey*:

Dylan, Vernon and Daniel Jones at The Garth, Pennard, Summer, 1951.
' . . . a short dramatic entertainment . . . '

We had reached the last gate. Dusk drew around us and the town. I said: What has become of him now?
Dead. The Park-keeper said:
(*The park bell rings*)
Dead . . . Dead . . . Dead . . . Dead . . . Dead . . . Dead.

We were soon snatching books from each other and reading our favourite bits of Dickens; when the bathers came back we looked up into the sun grudgingly. But Dylan went on being "nice". Apart from a short interlude of bickering with Caitlin, he "was happy all the time". Caitlin too was relaxed. She had been swimming, which she loved, children were romping about the grass but none of them was hers, a meal was going to be served which she had not had to prepare or serve (or indeed buy with non-existent money). Dylan and Dan put on a short dramatic entertainment, of which the plot, though thrilling, was not easy to follow: Dan was a Pharaoh, looking noble and aloof in a mummy-case (an old zinc bath stood upright on its large end). Dylan was an Egyptologist searching in tombs, and Vernon was co-opted as a rather sheepish grave-robber, whereupon the Pharaoh's mummy emerged majestic and sinister from his case. It was based, I think, on the old silent film "The Mummy's Claw", which all three performers had seen at the Uplands Cinema in their youth.

When that was over, the children were swung in turns in the zinc bath until the bottom dropped out of it, there was a kind of cricket with a badminton racket and a tennis ball, Dylan was swung high on the swing with small shrieks on every descent, and everybody wandered about eating prawns, sewin, *bara brith*, chocolate biscuits and ice-cream. Dylan ate everything, Caitlin went for another swim, and then the long afternoon was over. It was the last time I saw Dylan.

Vernon saw him on only a few occasions after that. He could have gone down to Laugharne as he used to, but for some reason he did not do so. I think perhaps he was made uneasy by the continual rows between Dylan and Caitlin. He could no longer pretend that the quarrels were not serious. Caitlin seemed by now permanently embittered by her life; and, although she made me uneasy and often indignant because of her behaviour in public, I was firmly on her side and against Dylan's treatment of her. Her life seemed to me intolerable. I thought mine was hard enough. I suppose the poet's wife has never had a bed of roses to lie on—but I had at least a permanent roof over my head, (though the walls under it were only wood and asbestos) and a regular, if small, income. And I thought Laugharne was the end of the world; it depressed me, it was so mournfully lovely and half-dead.

Vernon did, however, go to Laugharne once more, when, in the summer of 1953, Francis Dufau-Labeyrie was in England. In 1946 the translation of Dylan's *A Prospect of the Sea,* called *Perspective sur la Mer,* was published in *L'Arche.** In 1947 *Les Editions de Minuit* brought out *Portrait de l'Artiste en Jeune Chien* (for which there can have been no better translator than Francis, who knew Dylan, Swansea and the Welsh so intimately). He had in fact sent Dylan the typescript of his translation before it was published but got no reply. He wrote to Vernon in December 1946:

> I am glad Dylan and Caitlin stayed with you. I have given up every hope of ever getting a letter from him, even a letter of abuse when he sees all the irrelevancies of my translation! I take down the address you give me anyway, although I suppose it must be as transient in character as the ones I previously had.

The visit to Laugharne in July 1953, three months before Dylan was to make his last fatal visit to America, was in the nature of a reunion, and Dylan felt it so. Francis

*"About Dylan's collected works published by the SEUIL in 1970, I think I should mention that, at the beginning of Vol.II they printed a very poor and dismally pedestrian translation of *A Prospect of the Sea.* Apparently they were unaware that L'Arche had published my *Perspective sur la Mer* back in 1946 and their *Une Vue sur la Mer* . . . carries nothing of the inner movement, enigmatic and from deep below that pervades the original . . . for which I had had the priceless benefit of Vernon's and Dylan's own guidance." F.D.L.

remembers him coming out of the Boat House to meet them, saying over and over again, "Fifteen years! Fifteen years!" They were all happy, going to Brown's Hotel for drinks, back to the Boat House for lunch, looking out from the balcony over the bay and Sir John's Hill. Dylan asked about the reception of *Portrait de l'Artiste*, and was amused when Francis solemnly repeated the words of Georges Lamerichs: "Ce fut un succès d'estime". But soon the tensions grew. Dylan was asked to read some poetry, and he began (perhaps hoping to conciliate Caitlin) by reading one of her poems, which he read beautifully and which the others admired. Then, at Vernon's request, he read *Over Sir John's Hill*, giving it, Vernon told me, an inexpressibly moving elegiac tone, his beautiful voice softer than usual, especially at the lines

> We grieve as the blithe birds, never again, leave shingle and
> elm,
> The heron and I,
> I young Aesop fabling to the near night . . .

But suddenly, horrifyingly, the tensions erupted. When Dylan read the lines of the last verse

> . . . I see the tilting whispering
> Heron, mirrored, go,
> As the snapt feathers snow,
> Fishing in the tear of the Towy . . .

he pronounced the word as 'tare'. Caitlin abruptly put in "Tear!" (pronouncing it as 'tier'.) Dylan became—with some reason—furious. They screamed their own versions of the word back and forth, until Dylan, his face congested, bawled, "But, for Christ's sake, the bloody word is *there*—I wrote it!" and seemed about to attack Caitlin. Aeronwy ran away and Colum began to scream; and both combatants were sullen and resentful, not speaking to each other for some time after that. But Vernon and Francis were shaken, and went out for a walk along the bay. Vernon knew both the combatants better than to intervene, but the incident remained in his memory and he referred to it obliquely in his paper on *Eight Poems by Dylan Thomas:*

> Some have suggested that in the line from the nursery rhyme: 'dilly dilly' Dylan was punning on his own name. That is possible. But it is utterly wrong to read 'Fishing in the t*ear* of the Towy' in the last stanza as 'Fishing in the t*ear* of the Towy'. I once heard that mistake made by an actor on the wireless. How, I wonder, did he reconcile this to
> 'the tune of the slow, Wear-willow river', at the end of that last stanza?

When Vernon and Francis returned after their stroll, Dylan was in the shed at the top of the garden. They talked about *Under Milk Wood*, which Dylan was still working on: he said that although it had been read successfully on stage, he was not yet satisfied with every detail of it for print. Vernon praised the device in *Over Sir John's Hill* of assonantal rhymes which exactly correspond to the images described, such as hedges, heron, headstone; dilly, dingle, distant. "Only you would have noticed that", Dylan said, amused. And for a little while they talked about the techniques of poetry as they used to do in Cwmdonkin Drive and Heatherslade. Vernon said he thought *Do Not Go Gentle* was close in its language to the late Yeats, and he wondered whether in the last verse there was not a reminiscence of Kierkegaard, "a kind of transposition of Kierkegaard's learning that his father had once stood upon a hill and cursed God". Dylan only smiled and remained silent.

Vernon and Dylan met once more for a few hours in the week before he left for America and his death. Dylan described the libretto of the opera he planned to write for Stravinsky's music:

> The opera was to describe the holiness of Earth which had been devastated, leaving alive only one old man and his children. Visitors from another planet would come to take the children away; and the old man, who alone remembered the beauty and mystery of Earth, would try to describe them to the visitors and his children, who had been too young to know these things.

And then again they were talking about the tricks of their trade:

Dylan told me that the first line of *In the White Giant's Thigh* had taken him three weeks to get right; and for the *Prologue* to the *Collected Poems* which was the last poem he finished, he used over a hundred and sixty pages of manuscript. No work in the world was harder than the making of a poem, he said.

They talked too about how Dylan had held his father's hand as he died; and he quoted the first lines of his unfinished Elegy for his father (which Vernon was later to complete):

> Too proud to die, broken and blind he died
> The darkest way, and did not turn away,
> A cold kind man brave in his narrow pride.

After that it was time for Vernon to go. Dylan walked a little way towards the bus terminus with him, telling him that Goronwy Rees, then Principal of University College Aberystwyth, wanted to give them both honorary degrees. "I told him yes for both of us", Dylan said, chuckling. "I said you must be a Doctor of Law and I am going to be a Doctor of Divinity." Then they departed, with no hint that it was to be for the last time. Vernon wrote afterwards of that last meeting:

Yet, since his death, it is most difficult to write of Dylan Thomas with detachment, just as it was most difficult to think of him with detachment when he was alive. He had the faculty of immediacy, of making everything present, and of becoming a part of people's lives almost before he knew them; how much more did he do this when he knew them well. When he went on a journey theatrical stories about him, each one funnier than the last, began to accumulate; when he returned, all that theatrical scenery, those props, disappeared, and it was he, in his intense and essentially calm awareness, who discarded them. He was the serious survivor of all his myths. This is now more difficult to understand; for the man who, just before leaving for America for the last time, recited to me the first lines of his unfinished

ELEGY for his Father, and the man who, eighteen years earlier, had, in his house above Swansea Bay, opened a file and read his poetry to me for the first time, are inextricably bound in a personality from which time has fallen. The slight figure of the boy of twenty who read the first poems and the full figure of the mature, but equally shy, poet who recited the beginning of the ELEGY speak to me with a single voice.

CHAPTER ELEVEN: PARADOXES

Such darkness lives there, where a last grief sings. —V. W.

Although Vernon did not go to America until 1964, he had American connections and American friends. Constantine FitzGibbon, Dylan's future biographer, had been at Bletchley, and so had Robert Hivnor, a writer who lived in New York and, like Francis Dufau-Labeyrie, corresponded frequently with Vernon. Besides this, Vernon's first book, *Selected Poems*, to be brought out in America was published in 1947 by New Directions. James Laughlin was the head of this firm, known in America, as Faber's was in England, as publishers of the best poetry. Laughlin was very tall; after my first meeting with him, I asked Dylan if he found him as pleasant as I did. "Oh, very delightful", he said, enunciating every consonant with extreme bitterness, "I was always having conversations with his navel, asking it to lend me money, and it never would".

But in fact New Directions took on the arduous task of selling Dylan's work in the forties, when he was completely unknown in America, and did a very good job. James Laughlin wrote to Vernon in 1946:

> It is frightfully hard to get our public here interested in an English poet . . . Dylan's first two books flopped even though they had good reviews. People here had Auden and Spender in their minds, and these were *the* English poets, and that was that. Now finally Dylan is being recognised here. There have been a good many articles in the little magazines about him, and he has also gotten some good publicity from the attacks of people like the Society for the Preservation of Sanity in Poetry. He is now their number one target. We sold 1800 of Dylan's NEW POEMS, and we are printing 4000 of his SELECTED WRITINGS (which includes D & E) and I think we will sell them.

When Dylan made his first visit to America in 1950, Vernon was not greatly in favour of it. He recognised the need to make money, of course, but he knew that poems could be written only in solitude and silence, and he grudged the time that would be lost in travelling and social life. Later, when stories filtered back about Dylan's reckless behaviour in America, he began to feel anxious, and was always happier when Dylan was in Wales. Still he knew the value of Dylan's readings of poetry, and was glad that his stature as poet and reader should be recognised. He wrote to all his American friends before the first tour. Bob Hivnor wrote from New York in April, 1950:

> "Do you know any Dylan Thomas stories?" seems to have become a common question where the benighted literary people around here—and I suppose all over America—gather. It seems there are many and since they split up into new stories like a cell dividing soon there will probably be many more. A few:
> At a party in his honour at Harvard (or Princeton? or Williams? or Connecticut Womens?) Pieter Viereck, an interesting poet and a Professor of History, brought several of his books as gifts to Thomas.
> "Here is my book *Terror and Decorum*".
> Thomas, "Ahh." Complete indifference.
> "Here is my book so and so."
> "Ohh." More indifference.
> "And here is my latest book *Conservatism Revisited.*"
> Thomas: "Better it should never have been visited at all."
>
> He was asked by an old lady about political prospects in England and he replies, "All I'm interested in is *breasts!*"
>
> To a comely co-ed at Radcliffe (or Vassar or Smith) he says "Oh to be suckled at those breasts!"
>
> At one point he claims to be the only male British poet.
>
> Professor so and so says to him at a Railroad station, "I am Professor so and so of the welcoming committee come here to welcome you."
> Thomas, goggle-eyed and belching on strange beers, "I'm glad you're Professor so and so . . . I'm glad there's a welcoming committee . . . I'm glad you're here . . . I'm glad."

It seems your fellow-citizen is enjoying himself and enacting perfectly the academic American's idea of a poet being irresponsible, undependable, drunk, sexy—at least in word. I heard him recite once and his performance was very good—extraordinary—but a little on the romantic side both in delivery and poems chosen. He read quite a few Welsh poets but nothing of yours the night I heard him. There was an encore and the chairman asked if anyone in the audience had a request. Many were shouted up and finally one was chosen and a British accent piped up from the back, "Could you choose one a little shorter, please?" I saw him afterward surrounded by women one or two feet taller and got a glimpse of his fine head and face.

Vernon wrote back encouraging Hivnor to get to know Dylan; they did not in fact meet, but Hivnor sent back a newspaper cutting which referred to Dylan's saying at one reading that Vernon was the best Welsh poet writing in English. Oscar Williams, the poet and anthologist, who had helped Dylan by placing his poems in American periodicals wrote to Vernon also in March 1950:

We have been seeing a great deal of Dylan here. His readings are magnificent, and all America is in love with him. Unfortunately our distances are fantastic, and Dylan is having something of an ordeal in travelling from our east coast to west coast, stopping off at innumerable places between. But all the adulation he is receiving doesn't prevent him from being homesick for Wales.

On subsequent tours too he tried to keep track of Dylan's movements by writing to friends; but he never wrote to Dylan nor Dylan to him. A few days after Dylan had landed from the S.S. United States to begin his third American tour in April 1953, Vernon wrote to Francis:

I wish now that I had given Dylan your Montreal address when I saw him a few weeks ago. He is now in America and I don't know his address. Do look out for any notice of his lectures or readings in Montreal. I know he went there on an earlier tour, but this is only a 6 weeks' tour and I don't know whether it will cover Canada as well as the United States. Surely you'll read about it if you take a literary paper. Try to see him.

About the final tour in mid-September 1953 he had some reason to be anxious. Dylan had told him, when he and Francis visited Laugharne a few weeks before, that he had been having 'black-outs' quite frequently, and that he could no longer eat with comfort or enjoyment, and had sent away to a newspaper for an advertised diet-sheet. This last fact impressed Vernon most. He had been accustomed throughout their friendship to hearing Dylan complain of his asthma, his bronchitis, his gout, his gastritis, his tuberculosis; but that Dylan should actually take some action was unheard-of. At Laugharne, too, there had been, if not an elegiac, at least a summing-up note when Dylan talked about his work. "I know I'm good", he said. "I think I have written a lot of good poetry, but I don't think I've written great poetry. I think Mozart was both good and great." It sounded as though he were assessing a completed *oeuvre*.

John Malcolm Brinnin meeting Dylan in the same month, felt that "he wanted above all to come back to America, and that he *would* come back to America." Vernon felt otherwise:

> Dylan Thomas spoke of his last tour as a necessity. It was the only one he approached with reluctance. Yet he did look forward, when the period of intensive work in New York would be over, to working with Stravinsky. His intention was to complete the script of 'UNDER MILK WOOD', on which he continued to make revisions, and to handle the performances in New York; and then to go on to Hollywood where he would work on their projected opera. He was, when he left England, in the position of a man who had several difficult hurdles to negotiate before reaching his objective. Had he been well, he would have done this easily. As it was, he hoped that the short blackouts he had occasionally suffered during the previous months would not recur. The project of the opera filled him with enthusiasm. He had sketched out a plan of the libretto in his mind, and he had the greatest regard for Stravinsky. He knew that he ought to see a doctor, but he feared that the doctor would pronounce him unfit and cancel the trip.

Nevertheless, in spite of foreboding and anxiety, it was with a sense of shock and unbelief that, on the Thursday before Dylan's death, he saw a headline in a newspaper (shown him by a customer in the bank) saying that Dylan Thomas was lying ill in a New York hospital. As I remember, this first announcement said nothing about Dylan's already being in a coma; and Vernon, though apprehensive, certainly feared nothing more at that time than a major illness for his friend. But the next day's bulletin was more serious, and on Saturday, as soon as the bank closed, he climbed up Constitution Hill to see Dan Jones. Dr. Jones gives his own account, in *My Friend Dylan Thomas*, of the telephone calls to New York that were made, and of the comfortless reply that came over the Atlantic; Vernon knew that Dylan's life was in the balance.

In the balance; yes; but that one scale was inevitably descending was proved by a telephone call to Pennard from the *Times*. The caller asked whether Vernon would be prepared to write an obituary of Dylan Thomas, and I can still hear Vernon's anguished cry, ''But he's not dead yet!'' But he was persuaded to write the obituary, feeling, as he said to me, that he at least would ignore the myth of the Byronic wastrel and present a true picture of the poet he knew. He worked for most of Sunday, making and discarding drafts; when at last he had said what he wanted to say, he read it to me. After a silence, he said, ''This is the only thing I have ever written that I pray will never be published.''

All that day, as Dylan lay unconscious in New York and Caitlin was dragged away from his bedside to a psychiatric clinic on Long Island, and Vernon typed and discarded, with his children playing outside his study, in a house in Chelsea Ceri Richards had been reading Dylan's *Collected Poems* and illustrating some of them. He paused in this occupation to write to Vernon:

> Frances and I are very distressed over the dangerous news of Dylan—it appears to be really very critical—we only hope that by some miracle he will survive and come back to Wales very soon. It is a great pity he has to make these jaunts to the

U.S.A., although of course it is a great occasion to be working
with Stravinsky.

I have been reading from his *Collected Works* this weekend
and his trouble deepens the tragedy in the poems—also,
whilst reading in his book, I have decorated many of the pages
—if Dylan gets well soon (we hope so so very much) then I
think of sending him a copy complete with the drawings.

Ceri Richards had left Swansea to live in London, but
spent his holidays in Pennard. In 1945 he had been com-
missioned by Tambimuttu, the editor of *Poetry* (London),
to illustrate *The Force That Through the Green Fuse
Drives the Flower.* To respond to Dylan's poems was a
sure way to Vernon's heart, and he and Ceri became close
friends. Ceri drew and painted illustrations of Vernon's
poems, Vernon wrote poems and articles about Ceri's
paintings. They looked on nature and humanity from the
same viewpoint; both saw creation as praise, and both
were aware of the suffering and sacrifice that must make a
part of praise. Vernon talked a great deal about Dylan and
they made many plans to meet him, but somehow these
plans were never successful. Then, the day before Dylan
left for his final tour, Alfred Janes drove Ceri down to
Laugharne. Ceri described the meeting in a letter to Vernon:

> I am truly thankful for the opportunity Fred and Mary gave
> me to meet him—and to meet him at Laugharne—I liked him
> at once—I felt a shyness, for I was a stranger and come with
> some curiosity even though it was with warmth and admir-
> ation—and Fred and Mary were very old companions—I
> think we would have come to like one another very much and
> I would love to have had other meetings with him—but as
> you say Vernon—if I had missed him then, I would have been
> filled with regret.
> . . . I am very happy to have met Caitlin with Dylan—I am
> afraid there was a great sadness in Caitlin that day for she was
> worried at Dylan's departure. What a profound pity she
> didn't go with him at last . . .
> The Boat House home was a melancholy but very beautiful
> place—and according to Dylan he never saw many people—

well, it was rather remote—but he filled it with his resounding voice and friendliness, and Swansea too.

It was important to Vernon that the two people who meant so much to him should have met each other. When Dr. Daniel Jones comments on the "crazy irrelevance", on hearing of Dylan's death, of such a remark as "What a good thing he just managed to meet Ceri Richards", he misunderstands what Vernon was feeling. In fact this meeting was to have a great effect on Ceri and on the drawings, paintings and lithographs which he was to create in memory of Dylan. He wrote on hearing of Dylan's death:

> Since his illness I have read his work with much greater understanding for his tragedy sings more clearly in his work it seems . . .
>   O, let me midlife mourn by the shrined
>   And druid heron's vows
>   The voyage to ruin I must run . . .
>   Yet, though I cry with tumbledown tongue,
>   Count my blessings aloud:
>   and right to the end.
> . . . no-one has read him with more love than I—or your work —and to work for visual equivalents in response to your poems—I have tried to meet imagery with imagery and meaning with meaning.

But on that Sunday in October no love or thoughts of his friends could hold Dylan back from "the silences and echoes of the passages of the eternal night". He was going further and further away; and on Monday at midday he died. Vernon's obituary appeared in the *Times* on Tuesday. It resembled other *Times* obituaries only in that it was anonymous:

> . . . He approached the great masters of his art with an impudent suspicion, because from the first, he distrusted the academic approach. Yet, when they had walked with him through the furnace of his own imagination and emerged unscathed, there was no man who loved them more. Indeed, no poet of the English language has so hoodwinked and confuted his critics. None has ever worn more brilliantly the mask of anarchy to conceal the true face of tradition. There was

nothing God ever made that Dylan Thomas, the revolution-
ary, wanted to alter. The careful compounder of explosive
imagery believed only in calm.

. . . Yet there was nothing topical in his work. The most mistaken of its admirers were those who loved it for its novelty.
It was, even in its first phases, an ancient poetry, not rejecting
antiquity for the present but seeking, with every device of
language, the ancestry of the moment.

. . . It is likely that by his death the world has lost a masterpiece. What it has not lost is the work of a poet who was able
to live Christianity in a public way, and whose work distilled
it—a poet narrow and severe with himself and wide and for-
giving in his affections. Innocence is always a paradox, and
Dylan Thomas presents, in retrospect, the greatest paradox
of our time.

This is by no means the usual voice of the Thunderer,
nor was it in any sense a conventional obituary. Other
papers might print accounts of Dylan Thomas's riotous
life; here it was ignored, not for prudential or prudish
reasons, but because it was of no importance to the life of
the poet and writer. The *Times* obituary was acclaimed as
a tour-de-force, and has been continually reprinted. John
Berryman's reaction is typical of many:

I must thank you with all my heart for writing the *Times*
obituary. I don't see how you did it. Sickened by the one in
the *NY Times* I went up to Times Square next day to get the
Times, which I read with astonishment & respect. I am with
you absolutely as to the special importance of *Deaths and
Entrances*, and I am glad you went so far. He was one of the
greatest poets who ever lived. I want the piece known in this
country and showed it last night to the editor of *New World
Writing* . . . and *Partisan Review* will print it if you and the
Times will allow it.

When it was reprinted the reaction of reviewers was the
same. The *New York Times Book Review* of an anthology
said:

. . . there's no better or more definitive item in the book than
the unsigned but justly celebrated obituary of Dylan Thomas
which first appeared in *The London Times*.

Dylan's death was a crushing blow to Vernon, but for the moment he had no time to feel its full weight. Dylan had died intestate, and Caitlin and the three children were destitute. A fund was started in New York to pay Dylan's hospital and mortician's fees, and the expenses for bringing the body back, but it was clear that some long-term provision for the family must be made, and other fund-raising activities were put in motion. Dr. Daniel Jones, Alfred Janes, Vernon and two other friends of Dylan's called on the Mayor and read a letter to him from the sponsors of the American fund—W. H. Auden, E. E. Cummings, Marianne Moore, Arthur Miller, Wallace Stevens and Tennessee Williams—which resulted in the opening of the Mayor of Swansea's fund.

Reporters telephoned, letters arrived, there was a rapidly organised radio tribute to Dylan on the day after his death, of which Vernon wrote to Francis:

> I would have written before but all the time has been caught up in telephone calls. I was with Dan Jones on Saturday and he cabled twice and phoned the New York hospital. Everything that could be done for Dylan was done but the tragedy is that it was not enough to save him.
>
> I read poems of his and Dan spoke a short tribute and played one of his own short piano compositions in a wireless tribute to him on Tuesday.
>
> My dear Francis, how glad I am that you saw him again on that happy and beautiful day before he died. He told me that he found you 'just the same', and the reunion was good.
>
> Mrs. Thomas is wonderfully brave. I have rung Brown's (opposite) several times, and they say she is bearing the news wonderfully.

Apart from his natural desolation, Vernon was made very unhappy by the rumours, accusations, innuendoes and denunciations that burst out as soon as Dylan died. He wanted very much to know what had really happened. Fortunately Bob Hivnor, who wrote from New York as soon as he heard the news, gave him the address of John Berryman, the one person who was at Dylan's bedside when he died. Vernon wrote to him at once, and received an immediate answer:

> Of course I understand there is no question of curiosity in your asking. My god. I will tell you as much as I can in a letter. But the dreadful truth is that I have nothing to tell you that will not grieve you. I suppose it is better to be grieved by facts than by mysteries. It is certainly the most terrible thing that has ever happened in my experience. I can't expurgate it, either, writing to you as Dylan's friend, though of course you will when you pass any of it on, or perhaps you will feel as I do that the truth is what matters. If I don't put it well, forgive me; my brains are broken.
>
> He had been working too hard at rehearsals, was depressed and of course drinking. He was talking about the Garden of Eden. The last time I saw him conscious (not very) was Saturday, at Harvey Breit's: he was loaded, and hardly able to speak, though we had some talk about Ted Roethke's drinking. Monday afternoon he told someone that he had never been so drunk in his life as Sunday when he went through three parties. Wednesday night he was having mild D.T.'s in his room here in the Chelsea, and went into coma. Apparently now, at this moment, his mind died. Two friends who were with him got him into Emergency at St. Vincent's, and half a dozen people workt on him all Thursday. But after they got his organs into working order, there was really nothing they could do except maintain breathing & nutrition, keep him clear of mucous, and administer anticonvulsants: it was up to him. He was in continuous crisis for four and a half days until he died at about twenty minutes to one, Monday afternoon. He was never conscious for a moment and had no pain. One of his best doctors told me immediately after his death that there had never been the slightest hope; but of course we did not know that. They thought there was water on the brain . . . but they couldn't even be sure of that. His condition was so extreme throughout that all they could exclude was haemorrhage: a spinal tap showed there was none. Under prolonged coma of this sort, the likelihood of severe brain damage is so great that it ought to be impossible to be sorry that he did not survive. By a piece of the worst luck in the world (Caitlin was hysterical, she smasht an image and tried to strangle John Brinnin and had to be put in restraint, and everyone else who was at the hospital was downstairs) I was

the only one there when he died. His body died utterly quiet, and he looked so tired that you might once more have burst into tears too but your grief would have been general, for the whole catastrophe not for the moment.

. . . I wish I could say something to help your feelings. It is a fraction of something, I think, that he did not have to die, as some other great poets have had to die, under the impression that what they had done was not worth doing. But this will not help you much. It doesn't help me.

Vernon showed this letter, I believe, to no-one but Ceri Richards and myself; Berryman's description of the quiet, tired body was to have a strong influence on Ceri's designs in memory of Dylan.

Caitlin brought Dylan's embalmed body back on the S.S. United States (on which Vernon was to make his first voyage to America eleven years later) and the funeral took place in Laugharne on the twenty-fourth of November. Although Vernon (with great difficulty, for days off were not easily granted by the Bank in those days) managed to be present, he felt afterwards that it might have been better not to go. He very much wanted to see Dylan once more; I am sure that the pancake make-up and heavily rouged cheeks which Dr. Jones refers to in his book would have had no effect on Vernon; they would have been one more of the masks under which the real Dylan delighted to conceal himself. But, sadly, the last look for which he hungered was denied him: in the car which took him to Laugharne was Huw Griffith, who felt it essential to stop at every pub from Swansea to Laugharne, presumably in honour of Dylan. When the car arrived at Laugharne, the coffin was in the church and the service had started. At the graveside film and television cameras whirred so loudly that the words of the committal were almost lost. Vernon pushed one camera aside as it obtruded on Caitlin's grief, and its operator hardly troubled to lower his voice as he cursed.

Afterwards Vernon walked about Laugharne a little in the brilliant autumn sunshine, but wherever he went he had been with Dylan. When he went back to the Pelican House where Dylan's mother lived Mrs. Thomas seemed bright and pleased with the unwonted company and the eulogies of her son. At Brown's afterwards the atmosphere of hysteria, the squabbles and melodrama, the throwing about of drink, all seemed to him to have nothing to do with Dylan's death. At one moment Caitlin leaned her head against his shoulder; he kissed her gently on the forehead. It was for him the saddest moment in a bleak day.

After the funeral there were still memorial programmes; one by the Little Theatre at the Bishop Gore Grammar School, at which Vernon read *Portrait of a Friend,* and the much longer one at the Royal Festival Hall on February 14th at which Michael Hordern read Vernon's *Elegiac Sonnet.* Vernon could not go, and Ceri wrote to him about it:

> It was an interesting evening, but there were many parts where I felt the sentiment was wrong—the songs, music and singers were wrong and I was indirectly expecting a criticism of this sort from Dan Jones when I asked him if he had found it an interesting evening. But the moment was a wrong one, of course.
>
> Perhaps you don't think Dylan's poems are suitable for music settings—and I feel this is true for their content—deeply philosophical and his similies [sic] immensely pictorial and visual and the mode of utterance—well his own voice . . .
>
> . . . Anyway Betty Lutyens doesn't possess the appropriate spirit for it—Edith Evans as a reader was completely out of her depth—although she read the moving oration from Edith Sitwell very nicely. Emlyn W was good but not so good as in the rehearsal . . . His 'Visit to Grandpa's' was very good but the 'Just like little dogs' was not so good. R. Burton read Fern Hill very well, obviously he loved this poem and knew it inside out so to speak and that is very important. Edith Evans was a stranger to his work—and Emlyn Williams wasn't deeply moved by it. Hugh Griffith was really Welsh and good —but to listen to the voice of Dylan at the end reading And death shall have no dominion—was perfection proceeded [sic] by so much imperfection. That was very moving—very moving. The Excerpt from Milk Wood was very fine—Really marvellous . . .You would have enjoyed the occasion Vernon and I would have liked you to have seen my settings for it—I believe they gave it the right atmosphere—My curtain was in

glorification of Dylan and my stage decor more seriously suggesting his passing and flight away from us.

. . . we went to a small party afterwards—I said a word or two to Caitlin who was there. I was in a box with Augustus John but I don't think he could have enjoyed it as he might because he had left his deaf aid behind—but he was evidently glad to meet Caitlin.

P.S. Whatever would Dylan say or think if he was able to see what was happening—he would perhaps blow the froth off his celestial beer at us and say we blasphemed—and that we took his name in vain—but he would like it if he feels we do it for love.

Although the news of Dylan's death made a sensation in America and Britain, he was at that time very little known elsewhere (except perhaps in Germany because of R. P. Becker's very good translation *Tode und Tore*) That his name was known at all in France was due largely to Francis Dufau-Labeyrie's *Portrait de l'Artiste en Jeune Chien* and to Vernon's persistent praise of him to Alfred Vallette (whose grandfather founded the *Mercure de France*) and to Georges-Albert Astre, critic and anthologist, who both took care that reviews of Dylan's work appeared in the *Mercure* and in *Lettres Françaises*. Vernon wrote immediately to tell them both of Dylan's death. Astre replied:

Je suis confus de répondre avec bien du retard à votre longue et émouvante lettre! Oui, j'ai été absolument stupéfait en apprenant la mort de Dylan Thomas . . . et vraiment ainsi touché par l'évènement que si je l'avais connu, lui, personellement: j'avais eu l'impression, tellement rare aujourd'hui, d'un poète qui avait inventé un univers; (et d'autant plus, je l'avoue, que le "climat" gallois m'étant moins familier qu'à un critique anglais, j'avais éprouvé tout le choc de ce langage, de cette puissance visionnaire!

. . . Je trouve très regrettable l'ignorance des Français en ce qui concerne Dylan Thomas: mais on le d'écouvrira certainement un jour, dans une dizaine d'années!! (C'est toujours ainsi chez nous!)

But no sympathy, no praise of Dylan, could help Vernon

now. "For the lover, it is the night into which his beloved goes that destroys his heart:" and Dylan had gone into that good night he had so often written of. Ceri understood but could not help. "You must feel a very great emptiness Vernon as a fellow-poet", he wrote, "and as one who loved his craft and imagery and understood it so deeply, it must be a great loss—a very great loss".

But (perhaps to his own surprise) it was not the poet and craftsman that Vernon mourned. Others might regret the poems he would never write; it was his friend he grieved for. "The true tragedy of Dylan Thomas's death is that he died", he wrote. "Every other consideration is secondary to that." The poetry remains for ever; it was the vanished past he mourned:

> It is not this that leaves the heart's way ploughed;
> It is the shade the sun no longer flings
> Of one who touched the humble and the proud.

CHAPTER TWELVE: "TO MOURN THE LATEST DEAD"

You were born to a musical order, die
To a musical order; seek, then, seek
Notes that were true in the past.—V.W.

It can be painful to come to terms with one's own beliefs. Vernon had always felt that

> Death is an arbitrary division, and just as a poet writes for the dead, and for the unborn, as much as for the living, the true audience for poetry is found in all three of these categories.

It may be possible to make so confident a statement when those you love are alive, and when you love the great dead; but can you go on treating the three categories as more or less interchangeable when your heart is torn by the dreadful change?

At first it was only loss that Vernon could feel. Absence may be as much part of a relationship as presence, but it takes time to realize this. Vernon had heard of the death of Yeats "without a change of voice": the death of Dylan Thomas was to change the voice of his poetry for ever. He had always written to, for and about the dead; the elegiac tone of his verse was, he insisted, not something over which he had any control. The material for poetry "came" to him; except in the case of light or humorous verse, he could not choose it. Sometimes whole lines or verses "came", ready-made; once, a whole poem, which he heard as though it were recited to him. (This was *Griefs of the Sea*, the poem which Dylan had, by accident or on purpose, altered before its publication in the first number of *Wales*.) In the years after Dylan's death poems about him welled up from Vernon's imagination like blood from a wound. Hitherto his poems, though often based on personal recollection, had been in themselves impersonal. Now it seemed as though he were actually trying to recreate Dylan in verse, to bring to life again the man he had known. No matter that in the last years of Dylan's life the old intimacy had ceased; that blank interval was obliter-

ated and only the days when they were close friends were
remembered.

The first of the Dylan poems, evidently begun very soon
after his death, since it was published in May 1954 in
Botteghe Oscure, and Vernon was a very slow worker, was
Elegy for the Latest Dead. It was a short sonnet sequence,
which in early drafts consists of five sonnets each with its
own title. It breathes love and loss in every line. The first
sonnet is a meditation over the poet's grave, the second
has moved with the curlew to the Gower cliff-top where
the friends so often met. The third and fourth recall those
meetings:

> When first we met, this is the path we took,
> Exchanging thought, when, with a sudden look,
> He showed Earth shining like an open page,
> A myth in his live hand too young for age.
> His stubborn zeal transformed archaic skill,
> Binding young words old courses to fulfil
> Held by the curb of his unvarying soul
> Which kept all majesty in pure control
> While each excursion gave them fiery blood.
> Above this path, high on the cliff we stood
> That day, competing who could further cast
> A knife-edged stone. That knife-edge whistling past,
> Singing through air, hit rocks and water now.
> He crouched, and listened for the scream below.
>
> If the wrong world, if man's abuse of man
> Cast his own shadow on the race he ran,
> Here he forgot it. Here above the slade
> Sprang to immediate life his talking shade,
> The forward-looking shade accompanied
> By all the imagination in its greed
> Which, on the long, bare cliff-walks we enjoyed,
> With living shapes would dramatize the void.
> And I recall one late October day
> When, going to bathe, he peopled the whole bay
> (It was already dark) with human brutes
> Feeding in silence, in correct grey suits,
> Compact and patient, one with sanguine sighs
> Offering the next a sandwich of dried eyes.

But in spite of the momentary lifting of the heart at the recollection of Dylan's comic fantasizing, the sequence ends in almost pure sorrow:

> Yet, though all faded, still I count it pure
> To have loved the valid fact, made that endure
> Which held his heart and fixed the heron's eye.
> Who now says nothing says as much as I.
> Whatever books men write, when all is said
> There are no words to mourn the latest dead.

In April 1954 the son was born to Vernon who was to have been Dylan's god-child. Verse-making was once more the only way in which he could attempt to resolve the poignancy of his joy and pain. It was that year an early and heart-breakingly beautiful spring; already at the beginning of April the apple-blossom was in bud, the beech-leaves were breaking, the woodpecker darted about the garden, and Vernon watched his new-born child sleeping. This was the source of the poem *Birth and Morning*. The final version breathes through all its twelve verses a sense of bitter loss:

> I restore to the garden the footprints of one that was near
> Whose arms would cradle you now, a magnanimous ghost,
> But who sleeps without knowing your name in the turn and
>   the quick of the year.

An earlier draft in the British Library is yet more piercing:

> Who then, shall wake them, these the heart held dear? . . .
> Of the many whose names are in the dust, of the one I shall
>   name him by,
> While the apple-trees move under wind in the wonder of
>   morning,
> He nothing knows. Now the woodpecker, knocking, is near,
> But he does not hear, and a tear is all I know, or he, of the sky.

Another draft expresses not only grief, but the isolation of the grieving:

> That lies in earth about which the air knows nothing.
> In the dark there sleeps that which could tell the light,
> But those about me ignore it;

> These things are beautiful in themselves;
> They remember nothing;
> They exist in the mind of God,
> Nor grieve for that which is lost.

Birth and Morning forms part of Vernon's fifth book of poems, which appeared six years after Dylan's death. The title, *Cypress and Acacia,* explains its theme: the cypress is the tree of death, the acacia of life. The whole book is a meditation on the meaning of death to the living, many of its poems are concerned explicitly or implicitly with the death of Dylan Thomas. *The Curlew* is one of the most moving of these; originally one of the sonnets in the sequence *Elegy for the Latest Dead,* it turned into a poem in its own right:

> Sweet-throated cry, by one no longer heard
> Who, more than many, loved the wandering bird,
> Unchanged through generations and renewed,
> Perpetual child of its own solitude,
> The same on rocks and over sea I hear
> Return now with his unreturning year.

In the earlier sonnet these lines were more poignant:

> Alone I hear it now, alone I hear
> A curlew call the unreturning year.

A group of these poems, *The Sloe, The Return,* and *The Exacting Ghost,* describe the effect on Vernon of a dream about Dylan which came to him in, I think, February or early March of 1954. I well remember his agitation when he told me about the dream, and the uneasiness it caused him for months afterwards. Like many imaginative people, he dreamed often and vividly, but this particular dream had a quality which distinguished it from all others. He described it as being so real that the outlines of everything in it appeared solid; he could see the texture of the skin on Dylan's face, and the slightly greasy gloss on every curl, as though he were looking at a film close-up. He even saw a small mole on the side of the jaw which he did not remember to have seen in Dylan's life-time. Vernon was

160

not a superstitious nor an impressible man (he once said
that he could not imagine being afraid of ghosts), but he
was never able to decide whether this was an unusually
vivid dream or an actual visit from the dead.

The Sloe, which was the earliest of the three poems,
merely describes the strange sensation of the dreamer, seeing the dead friend's face with greater clarity than it was
ever seen in life:

> Too like those lineaments
> For waking eyes to see,
> Yet those the dream presents
> Clearly to me.
>
> How much more vivid now
> Than when across your tomb
> Sunlight projects a bough
> In gradual gloom!

This was evidently not enough to exorcise the dream's
power, nor, indeed, was the next poem, *The Return.* This
is a disturbing poem, comparing the atmosphere of the
dream to the terror of an air-raid. Its original title, when it
was first published in the *London Magazine* in May 1955,
was *The Return (of a dead friend who experienced an air-
raid with me).*

> I lay, pulse beating fast,
> While the night raider passed
> And gave each hovering tick
> The speed of dream.
> Sleep in the dead of night could make all quick,
> Reverse the extreme
> Outrider's task on thought's magnetic beam.
>
> What life-uprooting year
> Sent him, an envoy, here
> To set two states at war?
> I'ld rather set
> Those just names up both states are honoured for,
> Lest time forget
> He is a hostage since our eyes last met.

Now from that neighbour state
One who all war did hate
Came as a witness back
From that night raid,
To make a truce, there in the very track
Where wings had made
A single engine stop, two hearts afraid.

But the "truce" is not made; the end of the poem finds
the "two states" still unreconciled:

Why let two states at war
Destroy the mind?
Those eyes beneath a brutal metaphor
Can substance find
In all time spurns but cannot leave behind.

The long struggle to resolve the dichotomies of life and
death, good and evil, dark and light was, much later, to
take shape in the dramatic poem *The Ballad of the Outer
Dark*, a sequel to *Ballad of the Mari Lwyd*. But when
the two dream-poems still left him restless and uneasy,
Vernon wrote a third, the kind of poem he had not written
since that other poem of a dead friend, *Yeats in Dublin*: a
plainly factual, almost a narrative account. This was *The
Exacting Ghost*:

I speak of an exacting ghost,
And if the world distrust my theme
I answer: This that moved me most
Was first a vision, then a dream.

By the new year you set great store.
The leaves have turned, and some are shed.
A sacred, moving metaphor
Is living in my mind, though dead.

I would have counted good years more,
But all is changed: your life has set.
I praise that living metaphor
And when I sleep I see it yet. . .

162

In crowded tavern you I found
Conversing there, yet knew you dead.
This was no ghost. When you turned round,
It was indeed your living head.

Time had returned, and pregnant wit
Lodged in your eyes. What health was this?
Never had context been so fit
To give old words new emphasis.

If hope was then restrained by doubt
Or joy by fear, I cannot tell.
All the disturbances of thought
Hung on my words; yet all seemed well.

You smiled. Your reassurance gave
My doubt its death, my hope its due.
I had always known beyond the grave,
I said, all would be well with you.

You fixed contracted, narrowing eyes
To challenge my instinctive sense,
The uncertainty of my surmise
Their penetration made intense.

'What right had you to know, what right
To arrogate so great a gift?'
I woke, and memory with the light
Brought back a weight I could not lift.

In sleep the dead and living year
Had stood one moment reconciled,
But in the next the accuser's spear
Had sacked the city of the child.

Vernon was a Christian, but perhaps an instinctive
rather than a theological believer. He had felt rather than
thought about the dead, who had so far been to him either
dead poets, translated immediately into a "sacred metaphor", or the anonymous dead whose immediate reward
for lives of poverty or sorrow was Heaven. As a young poet,
he had written, in *A Prayer Against Time*:

> God, let me not know grief
> Where time is uppermost,
> Not though it handle me
> More wretchedly than all . . .

Now time was uppermost for him: he wanted to bring back again the time when Dylan was alive; the past was almost more to him than the present. But the dream broke up both nostalgia and sentimentality. Wherever and whatever Dylan might be, he was in some sense responsible for himself and his acts; the total dispensation from all accountability which all Dylan's friends had conspired to allow him seemed for the first time suspect. The disquiet generated by the dream was the source of the poem *Angel and Man*. Poems about resurrection by Christians deal on the whole with judgment, purgatory, reunion or salvation. *Angel and Man* is a dialogue after death, perhaps after the end of the world. Although the Angel promises that

> . . . All sighs are ended.
> The sleep of earth, the long night sleep is over . . .

the risen man (in spite, presumably, of his own resurrection) rejects the promise:

> I would believe you, but I cannot.
> Too much is hidden.
> I hear your speech, but when your speech has faded
> It is the earth that counts, where these men lived. . .
> . . . Let others be deceived.
> I know this for a place where footsteps halted
> And where each footstep knocked upon the ground,
> Seeking true consolation. Think of this.
> Spirits were laid here to whom some were dear,
> Who left them, sorrowful . . .
> I accept this for my portion. Grief was theirs,
> And grief, their lot, is likely to be mine.

It is a strange and uneasy poem. *The Mask of Winter*, too, is a poem that seems to equate winter with loss, and to find remote the promise of an eventual spring:

Until the waking bud
Forms on the sleeping tree,
By dictates of the blood
The dead admonish me.

I cannot separate
So soundlessly they shine,
The windings of past fate,
Nor the lost lives from mine.

Yet nowhere in this waste
Voices from time endure.
No footprint here is traced,
No dying signature.

No rain, no curlew-cry
Calling across the field:
The locked lane under sky
Is blocked with snow and sealed.

Again, in *Buried Light*, loss seems paramount and re-surrection not considered:

What are the light and wind to me?
The lamp I love is gone to ground.
There all the thunder of the sea
Becomes by contrast idle sound . . .

And men may find, beneath the sun,
Dashed into pieces by old wrong,
A relic, lost to nature, one
Whose passion stops the mouth of song.

The same sense of utter loss shows in the last verse of a three-verse typescript, found, with many other drafts of poems for Dylan, after Vernon's own death:

Who would have thought a single step
And voice could widow all the ground
And bring a garland to my sleep
Brighter than all the day had found?

In the Protestant Cemetery, Rome (whose first line, 'Where cypress and acacia stand' gives the book its title) is not explicitly concerned with Dylan's death, but there is no doubt that this was in Vernon's mind when he wrote it. The poem describes the graves of Keats and Shelley, each neighboured by the grave of a friend, Severn and Trelawney:

> And the paired friends, a space apart,
> Draw the leaves' whisperings, heart to heart.

It is impossible that Vernon should not have thought of his own friend's grave. These lines seem to me as much about that Laugharne churchyard as about Rome:

> How still the graveyard: one at peace
> And one so restless. Time must cease
> Before they understand each other.
> Yet now they do, for now their mother
> Casts on them her falling leaves.
> No longer the miraculous grieves
> For youth cut off, reclaimed by age,
> Where history sets a tragic stage.
> Character keeps its vesture on
> Holding the body, though it's gone;
> And the paired friends, a space apart,
> Draw the leaves' whisperings, heart to heart.

After Dylan's death, the myth machine gathered speed and rattled across America and England for the next ten years. Sometimes the cargo it carried was a grubby one: Dylan, said *Time* magazine,

> was a slob, a liar, a moocher, a thief, a two-fisted booze-fighter, a puffy Priapus who regularly assaulted the wives of his best friends, an icy little hedonist who indifferently lived it up while his children went hungry . . . Though he looked like a choirboy, he argued like a Bolshevik, dressed like a bum, drank like a culvert, smoked like an ad for cancer, bragged that he was addicted to onanism and had committed an indecency with a member of Parliament.

Dispiriting though such stuff was to read, it was no worse than the over-sentimentalized reminiscences of people who had once stood next to him in a bar or seen him waiting on the opposite platform in a railway station. John

Ciardi commented on the strange phenomenon of Dylan's power to create a sense of intimacy in everyone he met:

> . . . the country is sown from coast to coast with people who honestly think of him as an intimate friend, usually after no more than one or two drinks together. Something about the man involved people in him in an intensely personal way.

The picture of Dylan presented by both admirers and detractors seemed to Vernon more and more unlike the man he had known, and the poet seemed to be forgotten in anecdotes of the drunkard and entertainer. It was not so much indignation that Dylan's life should be cheapened, since Dylan never minded being misunderstood, and indeed often gleefully brought about deliberate misunderstandings, that led to *A True Picture Restored*, composed in 1954; the poem was a noble vindication, not of the poetry, which needed no vindication, but of the man whose life had been devoted to it. Dylan is given his rightful place with the great poets he loved:

> Nearer the pulse than other themes
> His deathborn claims are pressed.
> Fired first by Milton, then the dreams
> Of Herbert's holy breast,
> Out of his days the sunlight streams
> And fills the burning West.
>
> I look where soon the frosty Plough
> Shall hang above the sill
> And see the colours westward flow
> To green Carmarthen's hill.
> There sinks the sky of changes now
> On waters never still.
>
> Praise God, although a time is gone
> That shall not come again,
> If ever morning rightly shone,
> A glass to make all plain,
> The man I mourn can make it live,
> Every fallen grain.

The poem restores the "true picture" by painting lovingly

remembered scenes from the house in Cwmdonkin Drive, from Sea View and Laugharne, and from war-time London. There are oblique references to *The Hunchback in the Park*, the Laugharne poems such as the *Prologue* and *Over Sir John's Hill*, and to *Under Milk Wood*, but on the whole the tone is entirely personal: the bitter regret is for the man, not the poet, and it ends as it began, firmly rooted in Wales:

> Let each whose soul is in one place
> Still to that place be true.
> The man I mourn could honour such
> With every breath he drew.
> I never heard him wish to take
> A life from where it grew.
>
> And yet the man I mourn is gone,
> He who could give the rest
> So much to live for till the grave,
> And do it all in jest.
> Hard it must be, beyond this day,
> For even the grass to rest.

It is a tour de force, and was received as such when *Affinities* was published in 1962. One critic said:

> The poem has a ringing authenticity and a sense of awe which sets Dylan once and for all above the trivia of the Dylan-olaters and the academic assertions of the Dylanologists.

Louise Bogan, herself a poet of considerable stature, wrote in the *New Yorker*:

> Watkins steps into one well-lit center of contemporary interest with a long, beautifully written, and most poignant elegy . . . As Thomas's fellow-poet, compatriot and elder friend, Watkins describes the virtues of a young Thomas as they have never before been described.

The poem was also in some sense a catalyst for Vernon's feelings about Dylan's death. He still (and always) missed him and grieved for him, he wrote and talked about him continually, he was to write other poems about him; but never again one so personal, so intimately concerned with

a shared past. Even *To a Shell*, sad though it is, expressed
its sadness in metaphors.

The Present, about a photograph of Dylan which Rollie
McKenna, the American photographer, had given Vernon,
and which he kept always standing on his work-table, described the confusion of times we feel when we look at a
record of the past in the present which was then the future.
Again, the poem is sorrowful, but with a muted sorrow:

> Strange, is it not, that he for whom
> The living moment stood in flesh,
> Should bring the future to this room
> Held at arm's length, and always fresh.
>
> Strange, that his echoing words can spell
> New meanings though the die is cast,
> And tell us more than time can tell,
> Immediate in a timeless Past;
>
> And stranger still, for us who knew
> The living face and now return
> Its pictured gaze, so quick, so new,
> Love's vital fire being its concern,
>
> To think, though years should gallop now
> Or lag behind, he will not care,
> So calm the eyes beneath the brow,
> Held in a breath by angels there.

To the end of Vernon's life the shade of Dylan Thomas
continued to haunt his poems. In an early poem he had
said

> For the dead live, and I am of their kind.

It became in a way true. He loved life, but half of his
thought was always with the dead, and the past was as real
to him as the present.

> His name being said, instantly he appears,
> Caught, in a timeless flash, with life's own look
> Which none could seize or copy in a book.
> I marvel, who had missed that look for years.

And stranger still, for us who knew
The living face and now return
Its pictured gaze, so quick, so new,
Love's vital fire being its concern,

To think, though years should gallop now
Or lag behind, he will not care,
So calm the eyes beneath the brow,
Held in a breath by angels there.

[Original in possession of Rollie McKenna.]

The making and cheapening of the Dylan legend he always
scorned, and out of his scorn made the bitter little poem
Exegesis:

> So many voices
> Instead of one.
> Light, that is the driving force
> Of song alone:
> Give me this or darkness,
> The man or his bone.
>
> None shall replace him,
> Only falsify
> Light broken into colours,
> The altered sky.
> Hold back the bridle,
> Or the truth will lie.

But even grief has its death and its resurrection. The first
poem that Vernon had written in memory of Dylan had
been a curlew elegy, in which the bird's call carried
remorse across the sea, and, itself returning, recalled the
unreturning. Now, at last, towards the end of his own life
(the poem appeared in the posthumous *Fidelities*) he was
able to write another curlew poem. Here the call foretells
the end of Winter, and the poet is left, as the cry fades, to
turn to his work of creation. The poem is called *The Snow
Curlew.*

> Snow has fallen all night
> Over the cliff. There are no paths.
> All is even and white.
> The leaden sea ebbs back, the sky is not yet light.
> Hidden from dawn's grey patch
> Behind frosted windows, ash ticks out faded hearths.
>
> How quietly time passes. There is no mark
> Yet upon this manuscript of snow.
> Where water dripped, ice glitters, sheaved and stark.
> The pen has fallen from the hand of dark.
> White are lintel and latch.
> Earth has forgotten where her dead go.

Silence. Then a curlew flutes with its cry,
The low distance, that throbbing spring call,
Swifter than thought. It is good-bye
To all things not beginning, and I must try,
Making the driftwood catch,
To coax, where the cry fades, fires which cannot fall.

CHAPTER THIRTEEN: A TRUE PICTURE RESTORED

Time has no present till the past is true.—V.W.

Vernon was to labour all his life to restore what he believed the "true picture" of his dead friend, but he took it for granted that his labours would always be in verse. He felt that poetry was the language of belief and praise, while prose was the language of speculation, propaganda and rhetoric, for none of which he had much use. Dylan, however, evidently still exercised from beyond the grave his former powers of drawing his friends into his own orbit and embroiling them in unwished-for activities. Vernon found himself increasingly involved in undesired controversies, as counsel for the defence in literary indictments, as reluctant protagonist in arguments he disliked and resented.

The first spate of reminiscences about Dylan (always Dylan the "old ram-rod, dying of women", never about Dylan the poet) were beginning to die down when John Malcolm Brinnin's *Dylan Thomas in America* was published in 1956. It is difficult now to understand the hurricane of protest, recrimination and abuse raised by this book. Even at the time it came out I could see no reason why it should rouse such violent feelings. It was often inaccurate and careless in its presentation of facts, but the overall picture it presented of Dylan's childishness, compulsive behaviour and essential, if rarely displayed, charm seemed to me true enough. But to Vernon, as to many of Dylan's other friends, it was a betrayal of everything they believed about him, and Brinnin became the Judas to a Christ-like Dylan.

Vernon was sent the book for review. He was in a dilemma. He had always refused to review books by living authors, but he did not wish to lose the opportunity of saying something about the book which he thought ought to be said, and which had not so far been said. He comprom-

DYLAN.

I am going to begin by talking about Dylan Thomas because when I last came here he had just preceded me. I am not going to read his poems which he could do so superbly, but I am going to say something about the origin of a few of them and about the way in which he worked.

When I met him for the first time, just about 20 years ago, his first book was already printed. It occupied the entire front window of the best bookshop in Swansea, about fifty copies were displayed there. I went in and turned over its pages, on several successive days, without wanting to buy the book. I had the poems of Yeats, Eliot and Pound, and there was no other contemporary poet I wanted to buy at that time, except perhaps [crossed out] Auden. I did not believe in a poet learning from contemporary poets, but from ancient and dead poets. Also the poems of Yeats so dominated my imagination, as they came out, that I could not find room for another poet. I did, however, buy the book, and I made room for Dylan.

Soon after this he came to my house

One of Vernon's hundreds of pages of notes about Dylan.

174

ised by writing, at Stephen Spender's request, a non-review, an article entitled *Dylan Thomas in America* (published in *Encounter*) which made his views of Brinnin very clear indeed. An unpublished draft makes them clearer still:

> I was recently sent John Malcolm Brinnin's book for review, but declined, because I do not review books by living authors. Had I accepted, I would have been bound to condemn the book, in which I recognise two values only, the quoted words and judgments of Dylan Thomas himself, and the narration, in the last chapter, of the circumstances which led to his death. To call that death a self-inflicted one by any standards, and particularly by moral ones, is to accept the superficial tone in which the book is written, which is itself the hallmark of a superficial acquaintance and the prime evidence that its author did not know the man.

> *   *   *

> The tragedy of Dylan Thomas's death is made more bitter by the banality of judgment to which it gives rise. Those who were magnetised by his power to entertain became the victims of a mutually enacted delusion. The poet, simple, unaffected and true, was a person rarely seen by his audience whose dramatic spotlight changed him into what they desired. His stories, his wisecracks, they remembered, as who would not? But the surprising consistency of his judgments is one thing they never seem to have observed. In America his audiences recognised the superb reader of poetry certainly, but of the poet himself they knew nothing, or at least that is the impression left by this book. It might almost be said that he was killed partly by the grimace which responded to his entertainment and partly by the lack of any face which could see through it.

> To anyone who grasps this tragedy, whose final scene is horribly accelerated like a nightmare of misinterpretations on many levels, can anything be more cheap, tawdry and irrelevant than the carefully rendered account of everything the poet ate, or didn't eat, and drank? Can anything have less interest for any man on earth than the particular domestic scenes in which the author of the book exhibits the object of his mistaken idolatry to the curiosity of the world? It is certain that Dylan Thomas adapted his behaviour to his com-

pany, that he was willing to go a long way with any man in his imagination to explore that world, provided that it was a world which did not bore or disgust him. His instinct in conversation was to give, and to give prodigiously; and this instinct never failed.

* * *

To imagine Dylan Thomas as a teetotaller is a sad picture, and this he would not have become; but he was not an alcoholic either. Beer was to him a necessary social medium. Spirits were not; and it is my belief that this unnecessary adjunct, which is the medium of American hospitality, hastened his death. It would be comforting, I suppose, for some people to regard his record-breaking bout of spirit-drinking just before his death as a climax, a vindication of art against the world. Yet nothing could be further from the truth. Those who treasure such a conception of the artist are likely to misunderstand any artist, but particularly this one. It is their picture that is emasculated, not he; and it is to their picture that he has succumbed. His death is the death they would expect of such an artist, but his death is also, on other terms, his own death; and therein lies the tragedy.

A minor surprise of Brinnin's book is the almost complete absence from its pages of the people about whom Dylan Thomas was most eloquent when he returned from the tours. His enthusiasm for certain poets whose names hardly occur in the narrative had made the tours worth while. Everyone who reads this book should know that at least one other book, even on this subject, has been left out. His widow's introduction is sufficient to put readers on their guard. Besides this, there is an axiom that it is never possible to explain a poet's life. It is least of all possible in the eyes of one who builds upon the slender foundations of a late, business-distorted encounter. The eyes of a deceived photographer necessarily prepare the artificial pose. He sells to the world, without knowing it, a picture, or pictures, of a person who does not exist.

The poetry of Dylan Thomas and his late prose will remain his best interpreter. To the professional interrogator the task of meeting him involved the removal of many masks. He was himself stubborn, dogged and constant, fiery, combative, full of wonder, self-critical, compassionate, generous, trusting

simplicity through every complexity of mind, sociable, glad
of company, absorbed in all the mystery and extension of immediate experience. He was also extremely witty, and out of
a fundamental honesty drew, at any desired moment, enough
extravagance to illustrate his own myth. Even when the
myth possessed him he remained true to the values of his
imagination. Had he compromised with opposing values he
might, imaginatively, have had everything to die for; instead,
he had everything to live for, when he died.

The article was, like the poem *A True Picture Restored*,
exceptionally personal. On the whole, Vernon tended to
reveal only his opinions in public; here he revealed, more
perhaps than he realised, his feelings. His jealousy of Brinnin shows clearly in those descriptions of him as "one who
builds upon the slender foundations of a late, business-
distorted encounter", and the references to "the super-
ficial tone in which the book is written" as "prime
evidence that its author did not know the man." It was
always difficult, if not impossible, for Vernon to accept
that there really was another Dylan, or at least another
side to Dylan, never known by him at all—perhaps deliberately concealed from him. His insistence that the good
qualities he knew so well were the only qualities making
up Dylan's character, made him sometimes, as here,
unjust to those who perceived and were bewildered by the
negative side of genius. He consistently refused to accept
the fact of Dylan's infidelity to Caitlin, until, in America,
he was confronted with irrefutable proof; he then dis-
missed it by saying that "all those women were really
Caitlin to him". It may have been in a sense true; but it did
not change the fact.

Vernon never ceased to feel bitterly about *Dylan
Thomas in America* and its author; but, to confront himself with the picture of the Dylan he remembered, he
assembled all Dylan's letters to him, and read them
through for the first time since Dylan's death. For the first
time he conceived the idea of publishing them. He had resisted all attempts by American dealers to buy them (and
one attempt to steal them was unsuccessful), and had

never had any intention of making them public. But his re-reading convinced him that there was in them a great deal of material which would be of the greatest value to scholars and lovers of Dylan's poetry. Still undecided, he sent the letters to T. S. Eliot for an unbiased opinion. Eliot and Charles Monteith both felt that they should be published, and Vernon asked the Trustees of the Dylan Thomas estate for their permission. The Trustees replied that permission would be granted only on condition that Dent, Dylan's publishers, should bring out the book. Vernon dug in his heels immediately; a firm that had published Brinnin, he said, should never publish the letters he owned. There was a complete impasse.

But Dent wanted to publish the letters. David Higham, Dylan's agent and one of the Trustees, wrote to Vernon on April 23rd, 1956:

> I saw Stuart last week and he told me he had discussed with you my letter to him. I understand from him that you assented generally to the views I expressed, but feel reluctant about letting Dent have the book for the simple reason that they are publishing Brinnin's book . . .
>
> When this book by Brinnin came into my hands I had to recognise that no one had the power to stop its publication. In America it could be published without regard to any law of libel as we understand it and even here only minor modifications need have been made to make the book safe for a publisher who was prepared to take a reasonable risk of action. On the other hand, the book did and does contain a few pieces of work which is Dylan's copyright which are useful to it. I saw the opportunity for obtaining an assurance from the publishers here and in America that they would print the book with a disclaimer by Caitlin at the start.
>
> I also made quite sure that Caitlin should see the book before any further step was taken and she did in fact read it and assented to its publication provided that her disclaimer was printed with it . . . We even secured that this disclaimer should be printed with the extracts used serially in America. It seemed to me that if the book was to be published here, and we could not possibly prevent it being published, it was far better for Dent's to have it since as Dylan's own publishers

they would handle it with far more dignity and restraint than any other house . . .

I believe that to permit this publication is the right policy . . . If we as Dylan's Trustees—and of course I consulted the others—make any effort to suppress what someone thinks is the truth about Dylan there will inevitably arise rumours that there is something to be suppressed. The result of the publication of this book is going to be, you know, the exposure of Brinnin rather than Dylan to the public view; and in the interests of truth I think that is no bad thing, do you? . . . But whatever you think of the Trustees' policy, it is no more than fair to Dent that I should explain how they come into it. I think that whatever views you may have, you must hold them blameless.

Let me hear what you think, and whether you now believe that we could go ahead with Dylan's letters to you and with Dent. I quite understand that your sending them to Eliot was in no sense an offer to Faber but merely a submission to him personally.

But Vernon was unconvinced. On April 24th (mails rarely took longer than twenty-four hours in those days) he replied:

I am quite sure that in deciding to accept Brinnin's book for publication by Dent . . . you acted with the best of motives . . . I was, however, shocked that in this country it should be accepted by the same publishers who printed the 'COLLECT-ED POEMS'. My own instinct would have been to turn it down, not on the grounds of suppressing the truth, but on the grounds of its total inability to state it.

You are right in saying that I sent the letters to Eliot as a matter of personal interest, and not with a view to early publication. I did, at the same time, want to know whether in his opinion they would form a self-contained book, as I realised that sooner or later a decision about this would have to be made; and I thought that his opinion, as a person of great judgment and not particularly predisposed to favour Dylan's work, would be valuable. He did appreciate the letters, at first with some reservation, but later, I think, with complete enthusiasm; and Charles Monteith agreed with him that they would form an excellent book.

The position, therefore, is this: Faber's have taken up the

suggestion of printing these letters as a separate book and, rather to my surprise, they would like to publish them soon. To this I am agreeable. Such a separate publication before a definitive edition of letters by the regular publisher has many precedents, the most recent perhaps being Yeats' Letters to Dorothy Wellesley published by the Oxford Press before the Macmillan edition . . . Faber's are in my view the best publishers for the book. The book is already virtually accepted by them, subject to the approval of the Trustees.

If the Trustees are not willing to let Faber's have the book there remain two alternatives: either the letters are not to be published at all or they may be offered to Dent's at some future time. I am quite agreeable to the first alternative. The publication of Brinnin's book has compelled me to oppose the second. I have quite made up my mind about this. Faber's may have the book now. If they do not, Dent's will not have it until some time after their own book of miscellaneous letters has appeared.

All three parties now stood firm, each on his own strong point—Vernon that he would not release the letters for publication except to Faber, the Trustees that they would give permission for publication only to Dent, and Faber that Vernon would release the letters only to them. The cold war continued for many months, but eventually a kind of thaw set in, proceeding naturally enough from Faber and Dent, who were both extremely anxious to publish the letters. On 18th December, 1956 Peter du Sautoy, one of the Faber directors, wrote to Vernon:

We are on the point of concluding agreements both with Dents and with the Dylan Thomas trustees for the publication of Dylan Thomas's letters to you . . . The publication to be a joint one over the imprint of Dent and ourselves.

*   *   *

You may have heard the arrangements that we have made with Dents. We are going to produce the book and they are going to be responsible for selling it. Of course we shall each of us announce it in our own catalogues, but it seems best to have that division of labour, which is clear and straightforward.

There seemed no reason not to agree to this plan, and the typescript was immediately sent to Faber, who passed it on to Dent for a libel report. This again gave rise to several bursts of correspondence which, Vernon used to say, it was a great pity that Dylan was not alive to enjoy.

The libel report itself makes splendid comic reading. Dent's lawyer expressed anxiety about the references to Dylan's hostess in Penzance as a "simple" person, the references to the military policemen drinking with the deserters they had been sent to arrest, and to "Alfred Janes' deficiencies as a letter writer." (". . . now I have decided to abandon the book I was going to write and devote myself to the life and letter of Alfred Janes.") He was also worried about John Davenport being called an "amateur" writer. So was John Davenport. He wrote forcefully to Vernon:

> The nineteen stone (17, actually), the musicianship, the *etc.* are all fine. It's the 'amateur' that galls. 'Bad' would be better, if less flattering. It was the fact that I was in the strict sense a professional writer that enabled me to keep Dylan & his family for six months. Failed poets become professional writers, like me; Dylan, God bless him, was the amateur.

Mr. Grey Morgan, of the Swansea Grammar School, was asked whether he objected to Dylan's letter of March 16, 1947 ("I . . . had to go and see a master . . . to find out how much of the school was burned. 'Bloody near all', he said; then, with a nasty sigh, he added, 'All except Grey Morgan.'"). The old man replied forgivingly:

> The anecdote is new to me. I was "tickled" and enjoyed the joke. To intimates it is a typical Dylan "leg-pull" and I cannot object to it in isolation . . . Your letter brought back dim memories of fixing up Dylan in his first job at the Evening Post!

A more serious matter was Dylan's account of the machine-gun attack at New Quay. Vernon wanted to print the complete letter, on the grounds that the case had been fully reported in the daily papers at the time of the attacker's trial. Dent and Faber were not so sanguine. Charles Monteith explained what was worrying them:

Quite apart from the libel danger, don't you think it might be
a good idea, on general grounds of letting bygones to some
extent be bygones, to suppress _____'s name? . . . Technic-
ally, of course, this would hardly diminish the libel risk at
all; though in practice it might very effectively reduce it, for
the institution of proceedings by _____ would inevitably
result in fresh publicity about this affair, in which his name
couldn't be suppressed. What is important is that you should
satisfy yourself that Dylan Thomas's account of what
happened is, in fact, an accurate one. I've no reason at all to
suppose that it isn't; but it might possibly be that the story
which was eventually established in court differed in some
particulars from D.T.'s narrative in his letter.

It was not until Vernon had done a great deal of research
—work which he hated—that Monteith wrote again to say
that Mr. Bozman of Dent and he had changed their minds:

Here I've got to pass on what will, I fear, seem a pusil-
lanimous opinion—but it is the unanimous and firmly held
opinion of Bozman and myself. We both think that all references to this case should be cut out completely. The reason
for my change of view is that I didn't realise until I read the
press cutting which you sent me that _____ had been acquitted. From charges of (a) attempted murder (b) firing with
intent to endanger life and damage property and (c) of having
intended to commit bodily harm, a jury completely exoner-
ated him; and I've little doubt that Dylan Thomas's letter
would be held to constitute a repetition of these charges
which the prosecution failed to establish . . . If you yourself
should feel strongly that the passage should be retained we
could go back to the libel lawyer for his further advice . . . I've
very little doubt, though, that his advice would be in favour
of deletion. It's a tremendous pity that the passage should
go,—it's lively, exciting and of the greatest possible bio-
graphical interest; it isn't, though, directly relevant—is it?—
to the shaping or evolution of any of Dylan Thomas's poems.

Vernon wearily wrote to Mrs. _____, whom he knew
slightly, only to find that she was now separated from her
husband, whom, however, he managed to contact after
some trouble. The gentleman, naturally enough, only
wanted the whole affair to be forgotten, and the whole ref-

erence to it omitted, which Vernon felt would make the letter meaningless. Mr. Bozman and the lawyer wanted the whole letter dropped. It took many letters and telephone calls to bring everybody concerned to an agreement that the passage in question should read:

> I'd have written before this but . . . and Caitlin and I go to bed under the bed.

This was *not* a satisfactory solution. It was the best that could be done, but it left Vernon feeling that an enormous expenditure of time and energy had achieved very little. He was also embroiled in a correspondence with Lynette Roberts, Keidrych Rhys's former wife, who passionately objected to a paragraph about herself which said:

> Lynette, who cannot read Welsh, is revising the standard nineteenth-century book on Welsh Prosody, and also annotating a work on the Hedgerows of Carmarthenshire. I hope she becomes famous, and that they will name an insect after her.

To avoid more indignant letters, Vernon cravenly yielded, and left out the entire paragraph. He was exhausted and exasperated; he had thought that he would need only to type, arrange, and annotate the letters, and write a foreword, but for almost ten months he had not been able to work on his own poetry, for which continuity was essential. He began to wish that he had never embarked on the project; he had so little free time, and he did not want to spend what he had in the kind of altercation and discussion of business detail which he detested.

At last, however, the galley-proofs had been corrected, the page-proofs were actually being set, and Vernon felt that he could at last start on his own work again, when something happened which almost resulted in the withdrawal from publication of the *Letters* at the last minute. David Higham, who besides being one of the Trustees was also Dylan's agent, had arranged with Dent and Faber that they should offer a royalty of 12½% of the published price to 4,000 copies and 15% thereafter with an advance on account of royalties of £300—£100 on signatures and £200 on publication. Higham's letter to Vernon in November 1956, explaining these arrangements, went on:

> The Trustees propose that this first £100 should be paid to you in full, they to receive the £200 when the book comes out.

Vernon had agreed to this, but when in February the cheque for the advance arrived, it was for £90 only—Pearn, Pollinger & Higham had deducted their 10% commission. All Vernon's pent-up exasperation exploded in fury. He withdrew the letters from publication. The ten pounds was nothing, but that Dylan's agent should, as he thought, take commission while he had done all the work, was too much. But David Higham refused to budge, and it would after all be Vernon's own publishers, not Dent, who would suffer, since they had undertaken production, and would have to pay for all that had been done up to and including the page-proofs. Faber persuaded him to allow publication to go on; but he did insist on an agreement with Higham that he was free to reprint his own Foreword to the *Letters* without the deduction of an agent's commission. The affair was unpleasant, and relations between Vernon and David Higham were never what they had been before. Higham may have acted within the law, but Vernon continued to feel that he had acted unjustly.

There was however one small circumstance connected with the publication of the letters that always gave Vernon unfailing pleasure. Dent was in some ways an unlikely publisher for Dylan, since, as a house, it was inclined to be, if not prudish, at least careful. Richard Church, Dent's adviser, confessed that he found Dylan's poetry "alarming", and indeed refused to include *A Prospect of the Sea* in *The Map of Love* because of its "unwarrantable moments of sensuality". It seemed likely then that, since Dylan's letters were much more outspoken than anything he wrote for publication, a good deal even of what was left after the libel lawyer had been through it would be censored. But in fact, Mr. Bozman, an anxious but charming elderly gentleman, allowed such explicit passages as ". . . the dogs piss only on backdoors, and there are more unwanted babies shoved up the chimneys than there are used french letters in the offertory boxes", but stuck, inexplicably, at the word "shit". Not only would he not allow the word to be printed, but he evidently found himself unable to enunciate it, and telephone communications from Bozman about "that word" were passed on almost daily by Charles Monteith. A typical bulletin in January 1957 read thus:

> *That word.* I've spoken to Bozman on the telephone about this and his own strongly held view is that the 'whole passage' should be deleted . . . I think what he means is that the words "I bow before shit" should be taken out in toto. Though I'm sorry about this and personally should be in favour of leaving them in, my own view is that it's too trivial to make a fuss about and that we should agree. My original impression was that Dents would be quite happy with "sh-t"; but apparently that was wrong.

Trivial or not, the controversy raged on, until Vernon, both amused and compassionate at Bozman's crescendo of agitation, allowed the word to be deleted.

The book of *Letters to Vernon Watkins* came out in the autumn of 1957. The English reviews of this book, which has become part of the critical equipment of every student of Dylan Thomas, were on the whole poor; no English critic appeared to realize the importance of the letters. And Dylan's letters brought out, as Dylan himself used to bring out, all sorts of strange emotions. Richard Church talked of his own responsibility for bringing Dylan Thomas's work "to a wider audience by means of the machinery of a great publishing house;" he talked about Dylan's borrowing half-a-crown at the end of his first interview ("In the circumstances, this was embarrassing."); he talked about his own activities as a judge for the first Guinness Poetry Award. All he said of the book of *Letters,* in a review in *Truth* of two and a half columns, was "Meanwhile, here are his charming letters to his old friend, Watkins . . ."

Stephen Spender, in two columns in the *Observer,* ran down Dylan's character, poetry and letters—a curious review that seemed to be motivated entirely by envy and dislike. Of Dylan's character he said:

> Acquire a reputation for borrowing money, getting drunk, sleeping around, and do any or all of these things for any and all. It saves time and answers so many questions that it prevents the real questions being asked.

Of the poems:

> ... with all the fullness of his rhetorical language, and despite his passionate mourning and praise, there were unexplained empty gulfs in Thomas.
> ... One could scarcely make a prose paraphrase of what is said in a Dylan Thomas poem without an almost total loss of what the poem means.

Of the letters:

> They are newsy and gossipily depressing . . . But, except when he reminisces about his childhood or Swansea, they consist chiefly of the Thomas stereotype. The epistolary relationship with Watkins falls quickly into a scrounger-to-saint pattern and gets stuck there. The frankness is all of the over-boiled kind. Disappointing.

Vernon was indignant at Spender's suggestion ''that Dylan Thomas was anything but the most generous of men'', and there was an exchange of short sharp letters in the *Observer*, in the first of which Vernon wrote:

> I foresaw that lop-sided comment might be made on these small items of borrowing, but I left them in. In their time and context they were significant, mattering so much to him, and not at all to me.

Although there were a number of reviews which commented on Dylan's borrowing from Vernon, this was the only one that Vernon replied to. He began to wonder whether it would in fact have been better to leave out all references to his small loans and gifts. It was a great relief for him to hear that Caitlin approved of their inclusion. She had sent him, on a postcard from Sicily, that was also a gramophone record, the following request:

. . . I wonder if you would be very kind and do me a great
favour: to send me a copy of Dylan's letters; as I am only just
nearly brave enough to glance at some of Dylan's stuff, which
I could not bear within printed eyesight before; and I don't
know where I can get it from in Italy.

I did enjoy seeing you again after so long . . . bristling more
than ever, were such a phenomenon feasible, with hedgehog
integrity. Become more absolutely than was ever conceded to
a muchmarried voluminous family man before, an authentic
abstract levitating sage. A pure undespoiled, flying high
above the squalor of roof tops visionary . . .

Weathering the winter in Sicily is a dark hibernation of exces-
sive light; hence my unnatural craving for literature.

Vernon was shocked that Dent had not sent Caitlin a
copy of the *Letters* and immediately sent one to her. She
replied:

Thank you very much for the book which I really do appreciate, and your excellent comments. But opening the pages of
that early life makes it come back dreadfully near, like the
day before yesterday; and my late life shrinks into putrid in-
significance. So much for my great banging of doors with
hollow echoes. I quite agree with you about leaving in all
Dylan's money borrowings which are an essential part of the
letters and make them more faultily touching.

Caitlin's approval was almost the only comfort that Vernon had that winter as reviewers almost unanimously declared that the letters should not have been published. The
Tribune, in a review headed *Stop the Dylan Craze*, said:

Mr. Watkins has published a lot of trivial letters about trivial
things, and it is a pity.

The *Yorkshire Post*, "joining", as it admitted, "in the
expected chorus of disapproval", agreed with the *Tribune*:

People antipathetic towards Dylan Thomas and his nest of
cronies will probably derive a great deal of satisfaction from
the publication of these letters; and even a critic well-dis-
posed towards the poet and towards the printing of private
correspondence generally, may feel a little taken aback by the
trivia of much of the material here offered.

The nadir was reached in a review in the *Observer* by Penelope Mortimer. It is a triumph (or rather a disaster) of bad taste and ill-breeding, without the excuse of personal dislike to justify it, since the lady knew neither Dylan nor Vernon. It was in the form of a dialogue between two persons of bad taste and ill-breeding equal to their creator's:

> "How can you possibly understand his poetry without knowing what the man was like? Do you know there were times when he had to borrow a 2½d. stamp in order to post one of these letters?"
> "But people borrow stamps all the time—"
> "We aren't talking about *people*. This was Dylan. Really, don't you see the difference?"
> "No. And I don't see any point in publishing these dreary letters, which only succeed in presenting him as a self-pitying, shiftless baby who couldn't do a thing for himself, someone who lived such a trivial, boring life that he sounds like a sort of cultured George Gambol."

John Davenport alone, in the *Spectator*, realised the value and the integrity of the letters:

> This book is justified by the astonishing unity of the material . . .
> . . . But this is not a book of sloppy reminiscence, but a book really of technical reference. Pages 66 and 67 . . . are a complete refutation of those who think Thomas did not know what he was saying or how best to say it. These are humble and illuminating pages. Nobody could be anything but the better for reading them, even if he were totally uninterested in poetry.

And there came a few words of praise from the *Mercure de France:*

> Ce livre est précieux à plusieurs égards . . . Aussi ces lettres sont-elles un document indispensable sur la création artistique chez Thomas et sur la genèse de ses poèmes.

Vernon, while still convinced that the letters were "the richest letters of our times", could hardly fail to be disappointed and depressed by their reception in England. But when the book came out in America in 1958, it was a very

188

different matter. From every part of the United States it
was received with acclamations by the critics, many of
them poets themselves. Katherine Anne Porter, in the
New York Times Book Review, expressed what most
Americans seemed to feel about the spate of reminiscences
which had poured out since Dylan's death:

> So many persons have looked at Dylan Thomas through
> themselves, it is a change for the better to have Thomas look-
> ing at himself through a friend, a good, faithful gifted friend
> who played it straight. Here are no perverse sexual motives,
> no wifely jealousy and rivalry, no literary hangers-on elbow-
> ing each other out of the reflected glory, no wistful would-
> be's hoping that a little of the genius would rub off on them if
> only they could get near enough. Oh, none of all that dreari-
> ness!

The *Letters* was everywhere favourably compared to Brinnin's book and to Caitlin's *Leftover Life to Kill,* and were
regarded by John Ciardi, in the *Saturday Review,* as re-
storing the picture of the dedicated poet:

> It is part of a Thomas pattern that the two biographies of him
> published to date have been more personal to the writers than
> to Thomas as the subject. John Malcolm Brinnin had been
> accused after Thomas's death by rumours as outrageous as
> they were baseless, and he unfortunately . . . seems to have
> been at least as much concerned to defend himself as to por-
> tray Thomas. Caitlin Thomas, following with her own in-
> tensely personal reactions . . . was certainly too close to the
> turmoil of Thomas's death for anything like a balanced por-
> trait . . .
> With such cross-motives at work it is small wonder to find
> that Thomas is lost in the shuffle, and inevitable that his
> more sensational antics should take over the writing. The
> letters to Vernon Watkins, close friend and admired fellow-
> poet, are most valuable as a first redressing of the balance.

The American critics seemed not only more alive to the
wit, charm and real worth of the letters, but they had a far
more sensitive insight into Dylan's life and character, and
the compulsions which drove him to his death. R. Phelps,
in the *National Review,* commented on the ''zest and

charm'' which Thomas brought everywhere and to everyone:

> There is even perhaps a clue here to the terrible question of
> why so bountiful a man was so little able to preserve himself,
> and died at thirty-nine. For in every one of these letters . . .
> there is the same inexhaustible wish to please. No matter
> what he is saying or how he feels . . . he is always turning
> somersaults, always striving to engage and delight, always
> exerting himself to be liked. This was his profoundest virtue
> —this need to take the trouble to reach others; but it was also
> his most debilitating weakness. Even a Welshman has only
> so much energy, and Dylan Thomas gave so great a prop-
> ortion of his to the art of making himself loved that, event-
> ually, there was none left for anything else; not even for keep-
> ing his body alive.

The enthusiastic acclaim with which the letters were
received in America caused a great change in Vernon's attitude to that country, and led eventually to his own visits
there, and to many valued friendships. He had at first
blamed the Americans for not taking sufficient care of the
great poet in their midst (forgetting that the poet had never
allowed anyone to stop him doing what he wanted). Now
he felt that perhaps the Americans were the only ones who
had really understood Dylan. He found a review such as
Donald Demarest's in the *Mexico City News*, which said

> . . . Dylan Thomas is his own best and most enduring wit-
> ness. The handful of meaning-charged and ecstatic poems he
> left will long survive both his detractors and sycophants . . .

nearer the truth than what had been said in the *Times Literary Supplement* or the *Observer*. Even the Welsh
reviews concentrated more on Dylan's wild life than on
his serious poetry. Vernon for the first time felt an alien in
his own country, and turned across the Atlantic to friends
whose feelings matched his own. There is no doubt that he
went to America partly because Dylan had been there. It
was not that he wanted to follow Dylan's steps, but that he
wanted to meet those for whom Dylan still lived. This he
did, and it was what made him want to return there. He

said to Dr. George Thomas in a broadcast in February 1967:

> They're very fresh out there. They have very fresh ideas of composition; they're very enthusiastic. If you read your poems, the hall is packed. They're full of memories of Dylan Thomas's readings and this is very wonderful.

But when offers for the actual letters came, as they were bound to do, from American dealers and institutions, Vernon hesitated. He found that he did not want the letters to go overseas, and in March 1965 they found their permanent home in the British Library.

CHAPTER FOURTEEN:
BEHIND THE FABULOUS CURTAIN

I am not too proud to cry that He and he
Will never never go out of my mind.—D.T.

In December 1955 Vernon wrote to Francis:

> Last month I went through Dylan's letters, copying them,
> because I found I had lost two or three . . .
> Then I was sent the manuscript notes of the poem Dylan
> was working on when he died: an elegy about his father's
> death. There were sixty pages of notes. I extended and com-
> pleted a version of the poem from these, and this Spender is
> going to print in the February number of *Encounter*, so do
> look for this, if it ever reaches your dark city.

He described, in a talk at Gregynog in 1964, the actual
labour of assembling the poem. He had promised, he said,
that the talk should be about his own latest poems, the
ones written or published since his book *Affinities*, which
came out in 1962.

> But I shall begin by reading the very last poem which Dylan
> Thomas wrote. He left it unfinished. He had recited to me the
> opening lines in Swansea in 1953, and three years later* I was
> handed all the manuscript work towards the poem, with a re-
> quest that I should try to complete it. By a strange coinci-
> dence this work, in typescript and manuscript, and running
> to more than sixty pages, was handed to me on the very morn-
> ing after I had spent more than a month copying his letters to
> me, a task which had occupied me most evenings until very
> late; so I had the advantage of having read Dylan's own
> writing continuously when I was asked to begin work on the
> poem. My first attempt failed. There were a great many ver-
> sions and a great many variants. A week later I tried again,
> and the various jottings Dylan had made, consisting chiefly
> of single lines or a pair of lines, fell into shape. In the most
> complete versions, which were typed, it was clear that he had
> reached the 17th line, with a number of alternatives; and

*But see letter to F.D-L., above.

there was a nest of alterations and beginnings at that point. I
was guided by the four prose notes he had made for the poem.
Where two lines came together in the notebook drafts, I kept
that order; but otherwise I did not respect at all the order of
the pages.

The only word used in the whole poem without justification from the manuscript was "plain" in line twenty-
three, to rhyme with "pain". Of the added lines sixteen
were as Dylan wrote them, and the remainder were altered
only by the inversion of one or two words. The provisional
titles *The Darkest Way, Too Proud to Die,* and *True
Death*** had been used in the preparatory drafts, but were
rejected in favour of the title on the most complete. In his
note in *Encounter,* Vernon wrote:

> In the third line I have chosen "narrow pride" as against
> "burning pride" although "burning" occurs more often than
> "narrow" in the transcripts; but it was "narrow" in that line
> that he quoted to me from memory when I last saw him.

The order of the added lines might of course have been different, and the poem might, if Dylan had lived to write
more lines, have been longer. But the completed poem, as
it stands, is valid and moving. Dylan's death was the end
of a very great deal that meant much in Vernon's life; but it
was not the end of everything. The two friends were still,
in a sense, engaged in poetry together.

But Vernon now, because of Dylan's death, was also
engaged with prose (the writing of which he had hitherto
avoided) to an extent he would have thought impossible
and undesirable before 1953. He was continually asked for
reviews, articles, forewords and other prose pieces; and
though he refused a good many requests, he seldom turned
down the opportunity to write about Dylan. He was in any
case assembling a series of notes about Dylan for his own
pleasure and use, incorporating everything he remembered about their friendship; he could often draw on this
material for reviews, but also the mere writing down of

**Perhaps remembering V.W.'s poem *Prayer for a Real Death (Lady
with the Unicorn.)*

what he remembered would bring up other incidents forgotten until then.

J. A. Rolph had been compiling a bibliography of Dylan Thomas's works since 1952; Dylan had told Vernon about what he called 'this fantastic project'; he would have thought it just as fantastic that his unmethodical friend should review such a professional—and in one sense, unliterary—book as the Bibliography. But Vernon made a surprisingly good job of it. Unmethodical he might be— the notebooks in which he kept records of his own publications were disorderly and often inaccurate—but his encyclopaedic memory for poetry and his loving recollection of every word Dylan ever said to him enabled him not only to appreciate, but also to criticize, such a meticulous production as that of Mr. Rolph:

> Future generations will not regard Dylan Thomas as a prolific writer. The exuberance and abundance associated with his work derived largely from his presence and conversation. The small number of his written books must be invisibly multiplied in the memories of those who knew him, for his company was itself a creative thing, releasing a stream of ideas. Yet he distrusted this exuberance, this leaping fountain of his imagination, and subjected it to the strictest control. Abundance which empties itself in work after work becomes purposeless without that arresting moment which examines the cause of its display; and it was this moment which interested Dylan Thomas: his obsession was with the motive force of nature, not with nature itself.
>
> With a loose, prolific writer the task of the bibliographer becomes prodigiously wide; a meticulousness is brought to bear on the work which is not always justified by its extension, for critical assessment is outside the work of the bibliographer; he cannot emphasize what he admires or leave out what he does not like. His task is to complete the pattern of the work, and the degree of excitement in the pattern depends on its coherence. With some writers the pattern is not seen until its completion; with others it is lost in the process. In an ideal pattern everything has value, and the interest is not only sustained, but deepened, by the experience of life itself. In a supreme example, like Yeats or Beethoven, it is at

once seen that the perseverance of the artist over a lifetime has enhanced the pattern and given to the last works an intensity made possible only by all that had gone before; yet even these works would not exist without the artist's willingness in absolute honesty and humility to start afresh.

After commenting on some omissions and some details which had escaped Mr. Rolph's vigilance, Vernon allowed himself a crack at *Dylan Thomas in America*:

> There is nothing irrelevant or misleading in the contents of this fine book. Those who feel that it is regrettable that the publishers use the dust-jacket to advertise the recent, and to this writer deplorable, book about Dylan Thomas's American tours, are able to discard it.

Vernon had always stuck to his decision never to review work by a living writer, although reviewing would often have earned him money when he was hard up. Now that Dylan was dead, however, he did consent to review books by or about him, again because he thought he knew, and would say, things other reviewers might not know or say. He wrote to Francis at the end of 1954:

> Dylan's book of broadcasts, "Quite Early One Morning" is out, and I expect you have it. They are extraordinary, and most rich. The American one, which is being sent to me, is more complete, I believe, than the English one which I reviewed for the Times Literary Supplement. I never do reviewing, though I've been asked to a lot lately, but I did review this.

It was a new experience for him to study prose with care, even Dylan's prose. He came to respect it, and to see not only that it was closely related to the verse, but that it had its own unique value:

> From his first beginnings, both in poetry and prose, Dylan Thomas had moved from a haunted, confused and symbol-charged shaping-place in the direction of the living voice . . . He never, however, lost his preoccupation with words, and it is doubtful whether any writer, cramming his work with life, joy and gaiety, has used words with greater cunning . . . The poetry was made by isolation, the prose by his social life; yet

they acted upon each other, and out of this conflict came a new and miraculous use of language.

But always his own sense of the living Dylan and of his death came upon him, even while celebrating his genius:

> It is impossible to close the book without regret, without an infinite sense of loss. Dylan Thomas as a broadcaster was unique. His place in sound radio was equivalent to Chaplin's place in the silent film. The depth and range of these talks is extraordinary, and extraordinary in its depth and subtle variations was the voice which gave them life.

Vernon always, when considering Dylan's prose, linked it to the poems. In a *T.L.S.* review of *A Prospect of the Sea*, he commented on the early stories:

> These four years [1934 to 1938] were intensely active ones for the poet. He used them to exercise and explore his imaginative powers, and to curb, as far as he could, their volcanic force, while his life moved from adolescence to maturity. The poems of *The Map of Love* testify to his triumph in that struggle, while the stories reveal the same imagination, but also the dust and heat. They are often directly linked with the poems, particular phrases, like "desireless familiar" in the story "The Orchards" which is found later in the poem "To Others Than You" in *Deaths and Entrances*, being common to both. They have, then, a particular significance as the quarry from which certain elements of the poems were drawn.

The same theme, of the relation of verse to prose, and of the relation of Dylan's nature to both, ran through an unpublished version of a foreword to *Adventures in the Skin Trade*:

> In the stories of *Portrait of the Artist as a Young Dog* he released the spring of bubbling life and comic invention which his friends had always known, though he had, until then, kept it out of his work. In "Adventures in the Skin Trade" the comic invention was directed against himself. He was a poet of tragic vision, but he was also a born clown, always falling naturally into situations which became ludicrous. Just as it is impossible to understand Lear without his

Fool, it is impossible to have a clear picture of Dylan Thomas
without the self-parody which appears in "Adventures in the
Skin Trade." It is a key, not only to something instantly rec-
ognized in his personality, but to something afterwards rec-
ognized in his tragedy and early death. . . . Yet, like everything
Dylan wrote, this intensely personal comedy was a part of
him. This unique fragment, half fictional though it is, carries
the unmistakeable stamp of his personality. It is real now
because it was once real to him . . .

Vernon's last published comment on Dylan was a Note
for *Poetry* in May 1961. It was called *Behind the Fabulous
Curtain;* the title came from the last line of Dylan's poem
Today, this insect, and the world I breathe:

My cross of tales behind the fabulous curtain.

It says in its few short paragraphs all that can truly be said
of Dylan, and I give it in its entirety:

It is difficult to explain to anyone who did not know Dylan
Thomas why any study of him must remain totally inadequate. It is equally difficult to explain why those who
knew him find themselves deeply handicapped in writing
about him. The quality he prized most was seriousness, and
he was a born clown; but was there any other poet of recent
times who could create so quickly an intimacy of judgment,
an apprehension of what was valid, in art and in life? That is
perhaps one of the reasons why strangers who met him only
once for a long conversation felt, after his death, that they
had known him all their lives. The entertainer and the in-
tellectual alike were slightly ashamed after meeting him as
he could beat them both at their own game, but if they were
humble they quickly recognised that he was humble, too.
The prig was his *bête noire*, the pedant a black-and-white
cross-word figure whom he didn't despise.

The variety of life and its abundance sang in his veins. He
was born to praise it, and he did so most completely when
war distorted it into every manifestation of horror. When the
war ended, his own war continued. He was, on the one hand,
enriched by the heroic comedy of people's lives, for he loved
people, and, on the other, fascinated by artificial pattern, for
the problems of form he had to solve in his last poems were

subtler and more intricate than any he had ever set himself
before. He found freedom in the late broadcast scripts, but
pattern obsessed him. In this late work the prose, with all its
humorous invention, was made by his social life, the poetry
by his isolation in spite of that, the isolation of the entertainer who has taken off his mask. A writer's mask can be
fatal to him, and it is certain that the image the age demanded
of Dylan Thomas was accelerated by his popularity. His in-
fectious humour deceived everyone but himself. His method
was not to retreat from the mask, but to advance beyond it,
and in that exaggeration remain completely himself. He
agreed readily with his detractors, and did not at all mind
being misunderstood. Then, in the private dark, his exuber-
ance was subjected to the strictest control. The public figure
and the lyric poet whose work began and ended in the Garden
of Eden came to terms, terms which no critic or friend has the
complete equipment to analyse.

After the publication of the *Letters*, Vernon was regarded as an expert commentator on Dylan's life and work. He
became the often bewildered and always harassed target of
hundreds of requests, varying from the simple "I am doing
a Master's thesis on Dylan Thomas. Any information will
be welcome" to the more complex "I am doing my Ph.D.
on Dylan Thomas and enclose a 40-page questionnaire on
the poet which I should like you to return immediately."
These requests always came from America; English students in the early sixties were either more diffident or less
enterprising than Americans, or had just not got around to
realizing that Dylan Thomas was the in-poet to do a thesis
on. Sometimes, if they were rich or had grants, the Americans came to Swansea. They descended on Vernon in the
bank often enough for him to be taken off the counter,
where the Americans, undeterred by growing queues of
Welsh businessmen unsympathetic to scholarship, would
go steadily through their 40-page questionnaires, carefully
writing down each answer in longhand.

Once Vernon arrived home accompanied by a steel mil-
lionaire from Pittsburgh, bearing brandied peaches and
Bourbon, and his young wife, who had begged for a trip to
Europe because she had heard Dylan read his poetry. She

tapped gamely about the rocky cliffs on her high heels (a
gold bangle with her husband's name engraved on it about
one slender ankle) and took down quantities of notes,
while her husband looked fondly and proudly at her. They
stayed at one of Swansea's oldest hotels, the Mackworth,
and the millionaire said, not complainingly, that the 'Mac
Worth' had not the simple comfort of Claridge's.

The University College, Swansea, asked Vernon to
supervise the thesis of a French girl, who was attempting
to study Dylan's poetry without any knowledge of Christianity or the Bible. Her parents were atheists and she had
never been inside a church. Dylan's many Biblical
allusions were completely lost on her, and all her scrup-
ulous scholarship was of no use. She carefully annotated
every reference, but would arrive for tutorial sessions
vocal with frustration. "You say, we shall this week study
Marriage of a Virgin, but 'ow can we study what 'as no
sense? He say here

And the shipyards of Galilee's footprints 'ide a navy of doves.

Now I 'ave look up this Galilee, and it is a province in
Northern Caesarea. What is to make of that?" On Vernon's advice she read the New Testament, but it made
little impression on her, and she could not see why it
should have so strongly influenced Dylan that he should
make constant reference to it.* "No," she said stoutly.
"In my opinion, this is a poet which look for the difficulty."

Many critics were saying the same thing. Explicating
Dylan Thomas had by the early sixties become an in-
dustry. But the charge that, at least after the early poems,
Dylan was deliberately obscure, could always rouse
Vernon to greater fury than any attack on his own poetry.
He would enter the lists of any controversy on this subject,
and a letter to the *Spectator* in September 1964 is typical of
many:

*cf. Dylan Thomas, *Notes on the Art of Poetry*: ". . . the story of the
New Testament is part of my life."

It is not always easy to shift an argument about a poet to a true level of enquiry, as the combatants forget that it is the poetry that matters, not what they say about it. Yet the old charge that Dylan Thomas intended to baffle and confuse his readers is not quite dead . . .

By the time he was thirty Dylan Thomas had acquired a mastery of the suggestive power of words unequalled perhaps by any of his contemporaries. He was also very resourceful, and he would use all the mechanics of composition, which he often called tricks, to serve his imagination; yet without accident or luck, that element which gives permanence to a work of art, he never found them completely satisfying. Had he trusted obscurity, he could have been much more obscure, and had he trusted the exploitation of language alone, the body of his finished poetry would have been much greater than it is. He trusted, finally, what lay beyond mere mechanics, and so was able to coordinate and transcend them. He was extremely patient in his search for what he wanted in order to match the need of his imagination: on the one hand he tested words tirelessly, and on the other his instinct waited on that lightning illumination which would extend or intensify the poem's imaginative truth.

The leap from the persuasive word to the unalterable one is usually abrupt, and nothing is proved by Robert Frost's study of a manuscript of Dylan Thomas where the rhyming mechanics for a poem were set down. To be left behind with these mechanics is an incomplete situation. The purpose of all revision is to arrive at lucidity without loss of content, and if the work becomes more intricate in the process, this only means that the intricacy was already there, but its expression was not.

Just as a poet can only be partially understood in his lifetime, he may well be misunderstood after his death. Dylan Thomas did not mind being misunderstood, but anyone who thinks that he aimed at baffling people or at obscure utterance, or approached poetry with anything but complete honesty, is more deeply mistaken than he knows.

When David Holbrook's book *Llaregub Revisited* came out in 1962, Vernon read it with mounting irritation. It seemed to him to be simply perverse, and he began to annotate it, but gave up in despair. ''To do the job properly, I should have to write a paragraph for every sentence of Holbrook's,'' he said. But it seems likely that at one time he intended to write at least an article about it, since after his death a sheaf of notes was found, containing a detailed refutation of many of Holbrook's contentions. Of the poem *There Was a Saviour* Holbrook wrote "Everything is left to chance and sound.'' Vernon's comment was:

> *Nothing* is. Both are *used,* every offer of chance or sound examined before disciplined selection . . . *All* Holbrook's analysis is wrong.

Analyses of *I Make This in a Warring Absence, In Memory of Ann Jones* and *In Country Sleep* are torn to shreds, and to Holbrook's comment on *Vision and Prayer*—"George Herbert and Thomas are at opposite moral poles"—Vernon replied curtly:

> Nonsense. Dylan's arrogance was also rooted in humility.

He found "grotesque errors in analysis" in *Do Not Go Gentle into That Good Night;* and of *Elegy* he wrote:

> This poem is about his father's death. Holbrook seems to think it is about Dylan Thomas himself.

The notes contain a final section evidently intended to demolish the claims of many critics to assess Dylan's work. It begins:

> *Handicaps of the Author in common with most of Dylan's critics*:
> 1. Did not know the man.
> 2. Has been misled by the legend of Dylan Thomas built up by those who did not know him.
> 3. Begins with a *false* hypothesis that Dylan Thomas was an arrogant, egocentric *enfant terrible.* This was one of Dylan's masks, but it is one that he discarded in writing serious poetry.

The idea of writing a book about Dylan and his work, always rejected before *Llaregub Revisited,* was never afterwards entirely abandoned. Vernon continued to add to the

piles of Notes on Dylan Thomas, and indeed the last
addition to them was jotted down on the train going
through the Rocky Mountains three weeks before his
death. It is jotted on the back of a Canadian Pacific
envelope (on the front of which is a reminder that a grizzly
bear has just been sighted) and it says:

> *Dylan.* His revolt at plundered innocence. His mastery, both
> in verse and prose, of the suggestive power of words. The
> pivotal, organic word forking two meanings in the context,
> the second proliferating in the imagination from the first.
> e.g. And dig your grave in my breast
> This device is less used in the later, more lyrical poems.

Probably Vernon thought that the retirement he did not
live to enjoy would give him the leisure he had never had to
write a book of prose. Meanwhile a great many other
people, who were writing books about Dylan, came or
wrote to him, often for help, which he readily gave, and
sometimes for photographs which he as readily lent. Bill
Read came to Pennard in the autumn of 1963 to look for
material for his book *The Days of Dylan Thomas*, and
wrote in 1965:

> I don't know how to thank you properly for all your gener-
> osity and kindness in helping me prepare the book . . . I think
> I have followed your various comments to me exactly—at
> least I have intended to. If you should note any error of fact or
> interpretation I would be very grateful if you would let me
> know.

Ralph Maud sent a copy of *Entrances to Dylan Thomas'
Poetry* inscribed:

> To Vernon Watkins, with thanks for his invaluable *Letters.*

William Moynihan inscribed *The Craft and Art of Dylan
Thomas*

> To Vernon Watkins: in greatest admiration of the poet & the
> man and in appreciation of kindnesses.

Vernon also helped Dr. B. W. Murphy, an American psych-
iatrist, with his thesis on Dylan, in which he analysed the

creative and destructive content in Dylan's work. Constantine FitzGibbon sent the typescript of *The Life of Dylan Thomas* to Vernon to be vetted before being sent to the publishers; Vernon sent him back fifteen foolscap pages of single-spaced typing containing corrections, additions, emendations, suggestions, most of which proved to be of use. When the book was published the first paragraph of the Acknowledgments read

> A very great many people have helped me with this biography, both by giving me information and by checking and on occasion correcting what I have written. Those whom I should most like to thank are Caitlin Thomas, John Davenport, Pamela Hansford Johnson, Trevor Hughes and, perhaps above all, Vernon Watkins.

Constantine later consulted Vernon about the selection of Dylan's letters which was to come out in 1966. Vernon had some correspondence with Lady Snow (Pamela Hansford Johnson) about some of the early letters, in the course of which she wrote:

> [Constantine] seems to have made his selection with humanity, and I am sure he will delete what is likely to be really hurtful . . . Dylan was often extremely unpleasant about his mother, whom he loved, and whom I loved. It is true that my mother was pretty bored with her when they first met, since Dylan and I were off to Gower all day, and the mothers had nothing to do but sit and chat . . .
>   You are the one person of whom I never heard Dylan speak with anything but affection.

This last sentence gave Vernon so much pleasure that I never had the heart to point out to him that, since Dylan had broken off his association with Pamela before he met Vernon, and that, on her own testimony, her subsequent meetings with him were rare or non-existent, she could not have heard him talk much about Vernon, if at all.

It was not only from America that the writers on Dylan came; by the sixties his fame had penetrated to the rest of Europe and further afield. Georges-Albert Astre had an article on Dylan in *Les Lettres Françaises* in January 1963, together with some of the letters to Vernon; and the notes on Dylan Thomas in *La Poésie Anglaise* (1964) owed something to Vernon. His copy is inscribed "Avec ma gratitude et mon amical souvenir." *Bajo el Bosque de Leche* is inscribed by one of its translators "con agradecimiento, admiracion y afecto."

In 1960 Roberto Sanesi's book *Dylan Thomas* was published in Milan. Vernon had met Sanesi a few years after Dylan's death, and this became one of the closest friendships Dylan brought him. There is a charming picture of Vernon in the chapter *Swansea e gli anni giovanili*:

> Il poeta di *The Ballad of the Mary Llyd* [sic], capelli completeamente bianchi, gli occhi vivi, con l'aria da ragazzo e lo strano, abituale gesto della mano ad accarezzarsi la nuca . . .

Through Vernon, Sanesi met Ceri Richards, and a long and fruitful association developed. Both Dylan and Vernon had presented the artist with many themes from their poems, and in 1954 he had held an exhibition, *Homage to Two Poets*, at the Glynn Vivian Art Gallery in Swansea. Sanesi translated poems by both Vernon and Dylan, and eventually published a book on Vernon's early poetry, *Taliesin a Gower*. Ceri did a series of sketches based on Vernon's translations of Sanesi's poems. All three collaborated in *Elegiac Sonnet*, published in the *Immagini e Testi* series by M'Arte Edizioni, Milan, 1970. This consists of two lithographs by Ceri Richards on a poem by Vernon, translated into Italian by Sanesi.*

Here is the poem:

> Over this universal grass the sky
> Brings to the grieving earth its great reward,
> And it was right to lay ambition by,
> The strongest will being deep and the way hard.
> This body sleeping where the dead leaves lie
> Gives back to trees from colours they discard

---

*Ceri Richards was later to make for Gino Cerastico Editore, Milan, a colour lithograph *Elegy for Vernon Watkins*.

The patient light of its own penury
Out of whose silence wakes the living word.
And we who wake, who saw the swallows' wings
Seeking the turning-point of their own cloud,
Draw to one place his love of vanished things.
It is not this that leaves the heart's way ploughed;
It is the shade the sun no longer flings
Of one who touched the humble and the proud.

The lithographs illustrate the "body sleeping where the dead leaves lie" and "the swallows' wings / Seeking the turning-point of their own cloud."

It was also because of Dylan that Vernon found himself to his surprise what he had least expected to be: a scholarly contributor to reference books. In 1963 Rainbird, Maclean brought out *The Concise Encyclopaedia of English and American Poets and Poetry* under the editorship of Stephen Spender and Donald Hall. The editors wished, they said in a letter to Vernon, "to make this book representative of the best contemporary thought about poetry by the greatest living scholars, critics and poets." Vernon had 700 words to summarize his thoughts about Dylan, together with the facts about the poet's life and work. Again, as in the *Times* obituary, his contribution was not what might have been expected:

> From the first, he set himself the task of remaking the language in terms of his own vision. His first book . . . revealed an idiom, new to English poetry, whose concentrated force was easily adapted to the correspondence he sought between sexual imagery and themes of vast metaphysical range. The stubborn originality of his verse derived from a singleness of vision, at once Freudian and biblical, which remained fresh throughout his life, as though his eyes still remembered the Garden of Eden.

Because, or perhaps in spite, of this tour-de-force, in 1963 he was asked by the *Encyclopaedia Britannica* to do the entry for THOMAS, DYLAN MARLAIS. This was a shorter and much more conventional, but no less unlikely, piece of writing.

After the publication of his first book, Vernon had frequently been asked to lecture or read poems. Whatever his subject, some reference to Dylan was sure to occur in every talk. After Dylan's death, the references became more frequent and more important. Of the hundreds of talks he gave till the day of his own death, in barely a dozen is there no reference to Dylan. His address to the Poetry Society in 1966 is typical of many:

> I have not time to talk about the extremely rich and searching imagination of Dylan himself. His poetry is *ancient,* as it is always dealing with first and last things. I remember acknowledging my great debt to him at Oxford in 1952. I had been reading my poems and had stated my belief that a true style can never be learnt from a contemporary, and a poet can only really relate himself to ancient and dead poets, and be influenced by them. At the end I was challenged. I was asked to reconcile this statement to my other one about the profound influence of Dylan Thomas. I said 'Dylan Thomas *is* an ancient poet. He happens to be alive.' This can no longer be said, but his work proclaims it.

Vernon's first visit to America came about entirely through Dylan's intervention. In New York in 1950 Dylan first met Theodore Roethke, whose poems he and Vernon both admired greatly. Dylan and Roethke discussed and read Vernon's poetry, and Roethke liked it very much. Years later, when he was Professor of Poetry at the University of Washington, Seattle, and was leaving for a sabbatical year, he asked Vernon to take his place. At that time Vernon was neither able nor willing to go to America; but Roethke's recommendation to the chairman of the English department was so strong that after his death Vernon was at last persuaded to become Visiting Professor of Poetry in Seattle. He commemorated both Dylan and Roethke in his poem *At Cwmrhydyceirw Quarry*:

> Yet grooves unwind voices; and he who engraves
> This stone, soon in his childhood's park to lie,
> Shall cut lines incised like a breaking cry,
> And give to stone that undulant line of waves.
> But who had guessed, in the hush of many graves
> Riven by love, it was Roethke's turn to die?

(The meeting of Dylan with Roethke in Seattle was in his mind only a week before his death, when he wrote the light poem *Arrival in East Shelby*, which includes the verse

> But what a stir and what a rumpus
> Ran from the station round the campus
> When Thomas, finger stuck in bottle,
> Taxi'd to Roethke in Seattle!)

It was in Cwmrhydyceirw Quarry that Vernon and the sculptor Ronald Cour found the blue pennant stone which now stands in Cwmdonkin Park in memory of Dylan. In January 1963 Vernon wrote to Francis:

> Tomorrow a television man is coming down from Bristol or Cardiff, and he will take me to Dylan's house or Cwmdonkin Park and ask about the absence of a memorial to Dylan in Swansea. Dylan hated ostentatious things, but a lot of people coming from all over the world have marvelled that there is nothing to show that he was born & lived here. So I think some lines, perhaps, will be carved, some lines from one of the poems, and perhaps set, unobtrusively, in Cwmdonkin Park but I don't know when.

The "television man" interviewed Vernon standing rather forlornly in Cwmdonkin Drive in the drifting snowflakes of a January dusk. He was cold from standing about, and his plea for some memorial to his friend was not as impassioned as it might otherwise have been; but the programme had some repercussions. A report of it reached New York, and on the first of February a cablegram was delivered to him at the Bank, addressed only to Vernon Watkins Swansea. Its text was as follows:

> Please allow us consider financing plaque honouring Dylan Thomas. Can you ascertain costs and write
>
> Caedmon Records

Vernon immediately wrote to David Jones to ask whether he would consider doing the lettering on any stone that might be thought suitable, and received on February 2nd the following answer:

About Dylan's thing: I think you had better rule me out, for I am not a letter-cutter in either stone or wood . . .

What I would suggest is that you or whoever is responsible get a good letter-cutter to do this thing *Er cof am Dylan*, I think it ought to have a bit of Welsh on it, if only that bit in place of *In Memoriam*.

After interviews with Swansea officials, Vernon wrote to tell the two ladies who ran Caedmon Records, Barbara Holdridge and Marianne Mantell, that the Town Council had given permission for a stone to be set up in Cwmdonkin Park. Mrs. Holdridge answered:

I cannot tell you how much pleasure it would give the two of us . . . to help in some way the perpetuation of Dylan's name. It is now eleven years since we first met him. In that time we have done everything possible to ensure the continuity of his voice in our world. If we can now do something else, to pay, in some small measure, our debt to Dylan as friend and poet, we shall be grateful. The plaque in Cwmdonkin Park is a sensitive and good thought. We hope that you will have it executed to your satisfaction, for we know that it will then be as we too would wish it. If the cost is not above fifty pounds, please don't hesitate to go ahead, and have us billed. If more is involved, we'll need to decide whether we can pay the extra amount also.

I hope that this happens. It would be such a good way to begin the year.

It did happen; but it took time, in spite of all that Vernon and Ronald Cour could do. But by September Vernon was able to write that the dedication of the stone would take place on the anniversary of Dylan's death, and Mrs. Holdridge wrote:

We did wonder whether the Dylan project was in the working stages, and we are very happy to know that it is now so nearly done . . . The simple stone memorial you have described pleases us very much, and we look forward to having a photograph of it beside the water . . . Knowing how much this memorial means to you, it would not be right for us to thank you for making it possible; but perhaps you will allow us to thank you for allowing us to have a small part in its fulfillment.

After the dedication Vernon sent the two ladies a photo-graph; it showed the water and the trees in Cwmdonkin Park, and between them the stone that was for many years to be Swansea's only memorial to its poet-son—set there, not by Swansea, but by America.

In January 1968, the magazine *Poetry* carried on the inside of its cover the words

VERNON WATKINS
1906-1967

and the editorial comment

> We learn with shock and sorrow, just as this issue goes into galley-proof, of the sudden death of Vernon Watkins . . .

In the same issue appeared the poem *Cwmrhydyceirw Elegiacs*. It shows that the stone in Cwmdonkin Park, and the quarry of its birth, were still in Vernon's mind a few months before his own death. The second verse is as fol-lows:

> Never shall time be stilled in the quarry of Cwmrhydyceirw,
> Not while the boulder recoils under the force of the fuse.
> Tablets imprisoned by rock, inert in the sleeping arena,
> Quake in the shudder of air, knowing the swallow has passed.
> One grief is enough, one tongue, to transfigure the ages:
> Let our tears for the dead earn the forgiveness of dust.

But indeed it is safe to say that to the end of his own life, the thought of Dylan was never out of Vernon's mind or heart. Among his papers were numbers of first drafts for poems, or single verses, or simply jottings, all for Dylan:

> Grief is too deep for one so young to bear.
> How could he keep his soul in patience here
> And calm, without that company of air?

and

> You that are gone from us, how well I understand you,
> Rising and setting, walking against the hour-glass while it
> > ran.
> Paid in your own true coin, with none to countermand you,
> Force, flourish and gift

Striking the eyes of the finder,
Making in death a silence akin to the living man.

and

Sorrow is more compelling than despair.
Who dreams that you are reached by violent ways
While these are nourished by the dread of stillness?
The best I knew still loved you for your calm.

But Vernon was also, in the last eighteen months of his life, occupied on a project which brought Dylan and himself closer than they had ever been. When he had completed Dylan's *Elegy* he had first deliberately involved himself, as it were, in the other poet's life and thought; but even so, he had had all Dylan's own notes to help him. The final result, by whatever difficulties it had come to fruition, was a matter of selection and arrangement. Now, in the summer of 1966, he attempted something much more difficult, and more intimate; he wrote the second half of a poem left incomplete by Dylan at his death.

In a broadcast talk produced by Douglas Cleverdon in September 1950 Dylan had explained that the three poems *In Country Sleep, Over Sir John's Hill* and *In the White Giant's Thigh* were parts of a long poem to be called *In Country Heaven*. A fourth poem with this title had been projected, but Vernon did not think that it had been put on paper. However, a fragmentary version, full of alternatives, and then in the possession of Mr. T. E. Hanley of Bradford, Pennsylvania, was sent to Vernon in, I think, 1955. In 1966 a copy of a much more resolved version, given by Dylan to John Malcolm Brinnin, was sent to Vernon by Professor William Moynihan. In this, eight stanzas were complete, and there were three lines probably intended as the first three of the next stanza. On this foundation, and remembering Dylan's exposition in the broadcast of the subject of the poem, Vernon improvised, "with no manuscript justification at all," another five stanzas and two lines. It is a remarkable achievement; it is not Dylan's poetry, but it is not Vernon's either. Read aloud, it is difficult to tell where the break comes; only at

the end of the poem does one realize that the tone and style
are different.

> Under the switchback glide of his tears
>> (And the salt light).
> Young Aesop fabling by the coracled Towy
>> Sees, dropped from nowhere, talons
> Rending, where herons stab for prey.
>
> He mourns rayed feathers branding the fox in flight
>> Strewing with cockerel phantoms
> Farms in death painting the arms of day;
>> Still in the silence of dew-drenched years
>>> Crowing proudly.
>
> He sings of Country Heaven's patience
>> (Dark with sleet spears)
> Building straw's breathing byre for the child newborn
>> Guarded from shafts of winter,
> Storing flowers' light in coombs and streams.
>
> Always through night, where the mountain face appears
>> In the ground cloth now withered,
> Tinder for fire, charred black, blood redeems
>> The thunderclap of warring nations'
>>> Flash, plumed with scorn.
>
> He mourns Heaven's countrymen in hedgerows
>> (Light is their shade!)
> Who ask what burned star, which of their turning homes,
>> Which world of magic spinning,
> Plunging from glory, self-destroyed,
>
> Whirled by betrayal, is cast from life, unmade,
>> Blasted from fledged beginning.
> The hedgerow rumour: 'Earth!' breathes on the void;
>> And they hold in their eyes green meadows,
>>> Streams, byres, and coombs.

Vernon sailed for America in September 1967, to teach a
course in Modern Poetry at the University of Washington,
Seattle. The poets he had chosen to lecture on were Hopkins, Yeats, Owen, Auden and, of course, Dylan Thomas.

But he lived only two weeks after his arrival in Seattle. His ashes were brought back to Pennard, and in St. Mary's church there is a memorial tablet, which, though it bears only the name VERNON WATKINS, is in reality a memorial also to that other poet with whom his life, even in the fourteen years after Dylan's death, had been so closely linked. It bears the words the one poet had written in memory of the other:

> Death cannot steal the light which love has kindled,
> Nor the years change it.

AFTERWORD

I hold from heaven the power to see what's gone
So clearly, that what is or is to be
Hinders no whit the noblest I have known,
His passion rooted, singing like a tree.—V.W.

Not many obituaries of Dylan Thomas made any mention
of Vernon Watkins. Every obituary of Vernon that I have
seen mentions Dylan, often to compare their poetry.
Philip Larkin said in the *Times*:

> He always stressed an affinity as a writer with his friend
> Dylan Thomas . . . Where Thomas was strongly wrought,
> earthy and even humorous in his poems, however, Watkins
> was abstract, rhapsodic and light in texture . . .

The *South Wales Evening Post* said:

> To few towns has befallen the honour of nurturing two poets
> of world-acknowledged eminence in the same generation.
> The friendship of Dylan Thomas and Vernon Watkins in pre-
> war Swansea is one of the most famous of literary affinities.
> Neither owed any measure of his fame to the other, but both
> benefited by their exchange of ideas on poetry . . . Yet their
> temperaments and ways of life were very different—Dylan
> the exhibitionist, bohemian and improvident; Vernon the
> quiet-living bank clerk, respected by all who knew him:
> Dylan burnt out at 40; Vernon, though eight years his senior,
> surviving him by 14 years during which his mystical thought
> deepened, his fame steadily grew, and his devotion to
> Dylan's memory never waned.

In the book *Vernon Watkins 1906-1967*, edited by Leslie
Norris, and containing tributes in prose and verse, twelve
of the eighteen contributors mention Dylan, but not one
attempts any assessment of the friendship. Hugo Williams
remembered

the unassuming way he assumed himself to be of interest—in

212

long, hilarious passenger-seat monologues—solely for his friendship with the ever-present 'Dylan'

and this was an impression Vernon also gave his colleagues at the University of Washington—that his sole justification for being there was that he had known Dylan Thomas.

Already in Vernon's lifetime the myth had arisen that Vernon represented a stable element in Dylan's unstable world. Dr. B. W. Murphy, in his *Creation and Destruction: Notes on Dylan Thomas* wrote about their relationship:

> It is timely to state how important Watkins was to Dylan, who depended on him in several ways. I believe Vernon was the ideal father of Dylan's family romance, and without his influence it seems likely to me Thomas would not have developed personally and poetically as he did, and may [sic] have disintegrated much earlier.

And in the memorial volume Glyn Jones commented on the fact that Vernon was prepared to endure forty years of routine in an unglamorous job to be able to concentrate on poetry:

> This sort of thorough-going renunciation Dylan, although himself incapable of any such single-mindedness, could understand and esteem, perhaps even revere. It is easy to see why he placed so much trust in Vernon and leaned so heavily upon him. In the mounting disorder of Dylan's affairs the serene dedication and the Christian acceptance of Vernon must have seemed like a still centre, a point of unattainable sanity.

Constantine FitzGibbon, in *The Life of Dylan Thomas*, perpetuated the myth:

> His friendship with Vernon Watkins was perhaps, from the point of view of the poet, the most important of his life after Dan Jones's . . . His relationship with Vernon Watkins was henceforth to be close and special . . . he provided the Welsh counterpoint to Dylan's roaring London friendships, but did so with an ease and flavour that Dylan's more provincial Welsh friends, such as Dan Jones, lacked. [In fact, Dr. Jones'

scholarship and knowledge of European literature were incomparably greater than Vernon's.]

Even Paul Ferris, though admitting that Vernon was "a strange friend" for Dylan, adds:

Watkins, eight years older, was a bulwark of some kind . . . a charitable, humorous man who teased out a quieter Thomas.

Only Roland Mathias in the *Writers of Wales* series, referring to "this odd friendship", warns about

accepting too absolutely the ranged reasons provided by the mature apologist for his friendship with Dylan Thomas . . .

Yes, and we must beware too of accepting the too easy interpretations of journalists and biographers. Dylan may have needed a father-figure, but he certainly did not want one, and would have run miles to escape from any "still centre" of "unattainable sanity". He wanted people who would supply his needs—money, drinks, amusement and company. He did not need any help with his poems, he had too much confidence for that; it was a bonus that Vernon would discuss technical details, type out the poems, and make him frequent, if small, loans. He kept in moderately close touch with Vernon only from 1936 to 1945, and certainly when I met him towards the end of the war I often had the impression that he was bored with Vernon's company. Of course there were times when he appeared to be affectionate, charming, solicitous; but there were many more times when he was irritable, captious, even rude. I am not saying this was not true for most of the people Dylan knew; I am only saying that I don't think Dylan was capable of a mature or lasting relationship (except perhaps, in certain ways, and for special reasons, with Dr. Daniel Jones). And the relationship with Vernon could never be called an intimate one. When they met, Dylan's engagement to Pamela Hansford Johnson had recently lapsed, but he did not mention her, nor did Vernon hear of Caitlin until Dylan was actually married. Indeed, Dylan never talked to Vernon about any of his escapades with women, certainly not of the woman called "Sarah", nor of Liz Reitell. Worse than this, he did not tell Vernon that so many of his early poems were taken from the Notebooks, though he had no hesitation in telling Henry Treece, who was never a close friend and whose poetry he despised.* He cared nothing about Vernon's feelings, leaving letters unanswered, never in the later years commenting on or even referring to his poetry, not turning up to his masque or his wedding. But this is only to say that Dylan was Dylan.

Why did Vernon, a passionate and in some ways unforgiving man, not only put up with this, but always come back for more? I think the answer is simpler than it appears. Biographers have commented on the differences between the two, but this was merely that they were wearing different masks. It was the same man underneath—or rather the same immature, confused, unresolved being, who had turned from life, which he could not control, to words, which he could. Vernon had merely chosen (or been condemned to, since neither seemed to have any real choice) a 'safer' or more conventional mask than Dylan. Dylan did not particularly care to see himself in a distorting mirror, but Vernon was always fascinated by the more dangerous path he might so easily have trodden. If Vernon's father had allowed him to spend the year in Italy he so desperately pleaded for after leaving Cambridge, he might never have gone into the bank. Might his poems have been better or worse if he had taken some of the risks his friend had taken? Dylan's life might tell him the answer; when that life ended, his chance of knowing the answer was gone for ever.

Dylan was his *alter ego*; when he supported, protected, admired Dylan it was because of the life he had never lived himself. Dr. Murphy comments on the extent to which Dylan's friends failed to recognise how sick Dylan clearly was. In Vernon's case, it was not so much a failure as an urgent unconscious need *not* to admit Dylan's many neur-

---

*"'In the beginning was the Bird'!!" he said bitterly to Vernon, of one of Treece's lines. "There's only one worse line, 'In the beginning was the Turd'."

otic symptoms, nor the increasing deterioration of his personality and habits. All this was perfectly clear to any unbiased observer. But Vernon stubbornly refused to see these symptoms of disintegration, or, if compelled to do so, refused to admit that they were serious; he called them part of the 'mask' Dylan chose to wear. That Dylan was increasingly helpless in their grip he could not, or would not, see. To do so, to take them seriously, would have been to admit the same tendencies in himself.

Vernon's mask was a different one, but it concealed the same guilt and immaturity, the same inability or unwillingness to cope with practical matters, the same dependence on other people to take care of him. He could not get into debt as Dylan did, because he would have lost his job at the bank; but he frittered money away, had no insurance, and made very little provision for his family after his death. He made a will only because he saw the difficulties Dylan's intestacy created for Caitlin and the children. He did not drink heavily as a matter of course, mainly because he could not spare the time to do so and still write poetry; but he did often get very drunk with Dylan. His progress to death seems to me as self-willed as Dylan's; he knew that he had had a serious coronary, but continued to play squash and climb up and down the steep cliffs of Gower, often dragging heavy objects such as fifty yards of fishing net or a sodden tree-trunk. The pathologist who performed the autopsy on him could not believe that he had been playing tennis when he died.

Dylan and Vernon were both terrified by the possibility of death, and both were helpless to adapt their lives in any way to prevent it; and both of them wrote poems about death to fortify themselves against the fear of death. Who knows how much alike they might have been if Dylan's life had been as closely structured by a regular job as Vernon's was, or if Vernon's life had been as totally unregulated as Dylan's? And who can say whether it was Dylan's death that made Vernon hurry on to death himself?

The quality in Dylan that Vernon most strongly asserted

was "rooted innocence." It cannot have been harmless-
ness that he meant, for Dylan, God knows, wounded,
grieved and sometimes damaged those he was closest to; it
must have been the helplessness with which he watched
himself live his terrible life that Vernon saw so clearly. It
was that helplessness, which he felt also in himself, that
held him so strongly.

For Dylan was like Robin, the marred anti-heroine of his
favourite novel *Nightwood*, whose face aged "only under
the blows of perpetual childhood", whose life was "a continual accident." The Doctor says of her

> "And why does Robin feel innocent? Every bed she leaves
> without caring fills her heart with peace and happiness . . .
> That's why she can't put herself in another's place . . . She
> knows she is innocent because she can't do anything in rel-
> ation to anyone but herself."

His friendships were in the end transitory relationships of
no real depth. But Vernon's feeling for Dylan was certainly
the most intense of his life; more than friendship, it was an
identification which did not end with death; indeed,
Dylan dead exercised an even greater hold over his imagination than in his lifetime. Memories of the past became
then so vivid that they seemed at times to blot out the present, and in brooding over them and over the strange dream
that showed him Dylan as a continuing presence, he began
to wonder whether the tragedy of Dylan's life had been
inevitable. He often regretted that he had not remained in
closer touch during the last years.

I don't think that in fact anyone could have averted the
catastrophe, certainly not Vernon. Dylan did need someone to discipline him; all his life he was like a desperate
child trying in vain to find out how far he could go, begging
someone to show him what the limits of his behaviour
were. But not one of his friends, however much they loved
him, was willing to do this. They all indulged him,
admired him, many of them even pushed him further than
he would have gone by himself, until at last he went too far
to come back. Our lives are often conditioned by what

people expect of us; nobody ever expected Dylan to live sanely—very few people ever even required normal standards of behaviour from him. Ordinary people had to be on time, pay debts, keep to contracts: Dylan was always indulged, laughed at, forgiven. It is very likely that he would have avoided any friend who did impose such conditions on him. And yet—I can't help remembering how perfectly he always behaved with Vernon's mother, who would certainly never have tolerated discourtesy or drunkenness; how meekly he put back Theodora FitzGibbon's sewing-machine (which he had hoped to pawn or sell) when she ordered him to, how industriously he turned in film scripts for £10 a week. It is a pity, perhaps, that the limits weren't set more often and more clearly.

Dylan's death turned the world round for Vernon. He "went with half his life about his ways", and the other half of himself was with Dylan. In 1966 he concluded his address to the Poetry Society (in which he talked a good deal about Dylan) with these words:

For the dead live, and I am of their kind.

INDEX

Agate, James, 68
Allen, Walter, 122
Amis, Kingsley, 33
Anglo-Welsh Review, 108, 113
Anvrouche, Jean, 63
L'Arche, 63, 137
Astre, G.-A., 154, 202-203
Auden, W. H., 42, 64, 142, 150, 210
Aury, Dominique, 63

Barfield, Owen, 23
Barnes, Djuna, 34-35, 88, 217
Barone, Carlo, 75-77, 79
Becker, R. P., 154
Berryman, John, 149-150, 152
Bible, 34
  Ecclesiastes, 13
  Isaiah, 34
  Job, 13, 34, 109-110
  Ruth, 34
Bogan, Louise, 167
Botteghe Oscure, 157
Bozman, E. F., 181-184
Brinnin, John Malcolm, 145, 151, 172-178, 188, 194, 209
Browning, Robert, 12
Burton, Richard, 153
Byron, George Gordon (6th Baron), 12

Caedmon Records, 130, 206
Cameron, Norman, 96
Campbell, Roy, 129
Church, Richard, 28, 31-32, 183-184
Ciardi, John, 165-166, 188
Cleverdon, Douglas, 209
Clinton-Baddeley, V. C., 124, 128
Corti, José, 63
Cour, Ronald, 206-207
Creighton, T. R. M., 37
Cummings, E. E., 150

Daily Express, 68
Davenport, John, 7, 89, 91, 95, 180, 187, 202
Davies, W. H., 28
De La Mare, Walter, 95
Demarest, Donald, 189
Dent, J. M. and Sons, 177-184
Dickens, Charles, 34, 90, 115, 134-135